Dedicated with gratitude to Dwight D. Eisenhower
for his service and devotion to America.
"Gently in Manner -- Strongly in Deed"

Managing Editor • Art Worthington
Publishers • Lawrence Siegel & Art Worthington
Designers • Peter Hess, Liz Howard & Marguerite Jones
Writing & Research • Laurie Cohn
Facilitator • Pamela Thomas
Series originated by Beverly Cohn

www.FLICKBACK.com
(800) 541-3533

Contents

Arts
&
Entertainment

Count Sarmi lines a silk crepe de chine kimono with flowery brocade to interpret the double luxury of "negligee pink" Soft-Weve, the bathroom tissue with the exquisite "facial quality" and delicate colors.

To match the luxurious 2-ply softness of snowy white Soft-Weve, Sybil Connolly of Dublin lavishes yards of crush-pleated Irish linen and hand-crocheted lace on this heavenly soft negligee.

Scaasi designs a younger-than-springtime "angel-wing" confection in Soft-Weve "negligee pink." *See* the softness, *see* how lovely Soft-Weve pastels are — right through their new transparent wrap!

The most noticed little luxury in your home

Soft-Weve®
2-PLY TISSUE BY SCOTT

SCOTT
soft-weve
FACIAL QUALITY
TWO-PLY TISSUE

NEW! "See-through" wrap

Fold on fold of silken-soft taffeta in a negligee designed by Count Sarmi to match "negligee green" Soft-Weve. See *all* the delicate colors with new Soft-Weve perforations, so neat and easy-to-tear.

Shimmery Grecian negligee — a slim, silvery vision in softest lamé chiffon. Specially designed by Yanni to match the heavenly softness of "facial quality" Soft-Weve in delicate "negligee blue."

With softest silk faille and satin, Ferreras creates a luxurious court-train peignoir strewn with French roses — specially designed to match the softness and delicacy of "negligee yellow" Soft-Weve.

movies

The Diary Of Anne Frank

A Riveting Drama Of A Jewish Family's Ordeal In Amsterdam During World War II, Leaves Audiences Stunned.

WORLD MOVIE FAVORITES

DORIS DAY & ROCK HUDSON

TONIGHT AT 8:30

GEORGE STEVENS'

THE DIARY OF ANNE FRANK

CINEMASCOPE
STEREOPHONIC SOUND
AIR CONDITIONED

RKO·PALACE
B WAY & 47th ST. PL7-2626

Tickets Available at Box·Office

DISNEY

Walt Disney's 7-years-in-the-making **Sleeping Beauty** *fails to recoup its production cost of six million dollars.*

METRO GOLDWYN MAYER
WILLIAM WYLER'S

BEN-HUR

Ben Hur, The Longest (3 Hours, 50 Minutes) And Costliest American Film Ever Made With A Budget Of $15 Million And Reserved Seats Going For A Top Price Of $4.00.

ARTS & ENTERTAINMENT

ENTERTAINMENT EXPERIENCE OF A LIFETIME!

-GOLDWYN-MAYER
presents
Tale of the Christ
GENERAL LEW WALLACE

BEN-HUR

Directed by
WILLIAM WYLER

CHARLTON HESTON · JACK HAWKINS

HUGH GRIFF

TECHNICOLOR

MARILYN MONROE
and her bosom companions
TONY CURTIS
JACK LEMMON
BILLY WILDER

NOT SUITABLE FOR CHILDREN

"SOME LIKE IT HOT"

O'BRIEN BROWN

Blue Denim
Breathless
Carry On Sergeant
CASPER'S BIRTHDAY PARTY
Cast A Long Shadow
COMPULSION
Crime & Punishment, USA
day of the outlaw
The Diary Of Anne Frank
THE FBI STORY
The Fugitive Kind
The Gene Krupa Story
GIDGET
HERCULES UNCHAINED
Hiroshima, Mon Amour
THE HORSE SOLDIERS
The Hound Of The Baskervilles
Imitation Of Life

1001 Arabian Nights
The 400 Blows
A Hole In The Head
AL CAPONE
ALASKA PASSAGE
Alias Jesse James
Anatomy Of A Murder
The Angry Red Planet
Aparajito
The Beat Generation
Beloved Infidel
Ben-Hur
The Big Circus
The Big Fisherman
BLACK ORCHID
BLACK ORPHEUS
The Blue Angel

a new kind of HORROR movie...
HORRIBLY FUNNY!

I WAS A TEEN-AGE BOY!

You'll love 'SHAGGY' the shaggiest of all shaggy dogs!

WALT DISNEY'S
the SHAGGY DOG

STARRING
Fred MacMURRAY · Jean HAGEN
TOMMY KIRK · ANNETTE FUNICELLO · TIM CONSIDINE · KEVIN CORCORAN

Journey To The Center Of The Earth

La Dolce Vita

The Last Angry Man

The Legend Of Tom Dooley

li'l abner

Look Back In Anger

The Lovers

The Mating Game

Middle Of The Night

THE MOUSE THAT ROARED

the mummy

NORTH BY NORTHWEST

The Nun's Story

Odds Against Tomorrow

On The Beach

Operation Petticoat

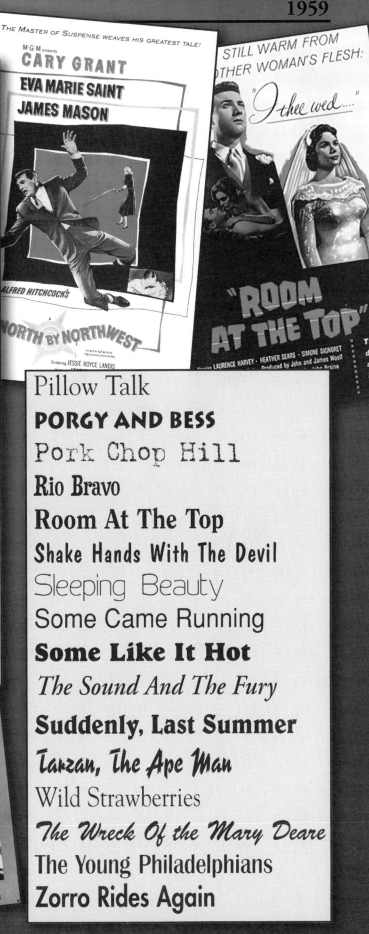

Pillow Talk

PORGY AND BESS

Pork Chop Hill

Rio Bravo

Room At The Top

Shake Hands With The Devil

Sleeping Beauty

Some Came Running

Some Like It Hot

The Sound And The Fury

Suddenly, Last Summer

Tarzan, The Ape Man

Wild Strawberries

The Wreck Of the Mary Deare

The Young Philadelphians

Zorro Rides Again

A NEW CROP OF HOLLYWOOD ACTRESSSES

MacLaine

Remick

Shirley MacLaine, 25
Hottest Actress In Hollywood

May Britt, 26
(The Young Lions)

Lee Remick, 23
*(A Face In The Crowd,
The Long, Hot Summer)*

Carolyn Jones, 26
*(Marjorie Morningstar,
Hole In The Head)*

Susan Kohner, 22
*(To Hell And Back,
The Big Fisherman)*

Diane Baker, 21
(The Diary Of Anne Frank)

Hope Lange, 26
(Bus Stop, Peyton Place)

STARS OF TOMORROW

Angie
Dickenson

Troy
Donahue

George
Hamilton

Tuesday
Weld

STARS WHO BRING IN BIG BUCKS AT THE BOX OFFICE

Wayne

Doris Day
Glenn Ford
Cary Grant
Susan Hayward
Rock Hudson
Jerry Lewis
Debbie Reynolds
Frank Sinatra
James Stewart
John Wayne

Day & Hudson

14

VARIETY ■ CLUBS INTERNATIONAL

sends a delegation, including Kim Novak and Perry Como, to visit President Eisenhower to mark the Club's 32nd year.

Ike joins 10,000 from show business who combine forces to aid their needy, raising over $75,000,000 through the years.

Ike receives a gold lifetime membership card from Variety head, George Eavey.

"PILLOW

ROCK HUDSON "PILLOW

DORIS DAY TALK"

TONY RANDALL · THELMA RITTER

Among the luminaries attending the East Coast Palace Premier are Ross Hunter *(top)* and U.I. President Milton Rackmil and his wife, Vivian Blaine *(bottom)*.

New York's finest *(above)* hold back the enthusiastic crowd as they strain to get a look at the film's star Rock Hudson who arrives with Tallulah Bankhead *(right)*.

"TALK"

Has Gala East Coast And West Coast Premiers

Sharing in the ovation is the ever-popular Thelma Ritter, another of Pillow Talk's comedy stars.

Meanwhile, Downtown, The New Murray Hill Theatre Is The Site Of Yet Another Showing Of "Pillow Talk" With Fire Commissioner Kavanagh Wielding The Axe To Officially Open The Theatre.

Novelist Patty Hurst (*top*), socialite Hope Hampton (*center*) and actor Tony Randall (*bottom*) all attend this gala benefit for the United Nations School.

meanwhile...

on the

Esther Williams and Jeff Chandler attend the premiere.

Rock Hudson just arrives by plane from New York for the debut of the comedy success.

Completing the picture is Doris Day, herself, *Pillow Talk*'s leading lady and America's #1 film star.

WEST COAST

INVITATIONAL PREMIERE

PILLOW TALK

THE HARVARD LAMPOON

PLEASE DON'T OPEN THE ENVELOPE

Kirk Douglas' performance in *The Vikings* wins him the not so coveted Harvard Lampoon's Worst Actor Of The Year Award for the third time.

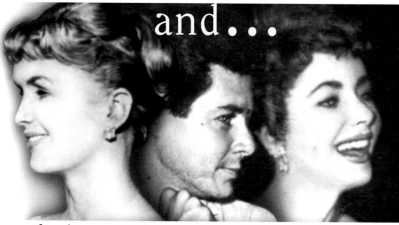

and...

...for the most entertaining off-screen performances, The Harvard Lampoon gives a special award to **Elizabeth Taylor**, **Debbie Reynolds** and **Eddie Fisher** for their marriage go round.

AhEAd By a NOSe

Theater owner Walter Reade, Jr. announces the premiere of an odoriferous film, nosing out Mike Todd, Jr.'s premiere of "Smell-O-Vision," a process developed for pumping a variety of odors into movie theaters.

Gregory Peck Declines Co-Starring Role With Marilyn Monroe In *Let's Make Love* Because The Parts Are Not Evenly Developed.

SOMETHING TO LAUGH ABOUT:

Jerry Lewis Forms A Comedy Workshop To Develop Budding Young Comics.

Purportedly the biggest deal ever made with an actor, Jerry Lewis signs a whopping $10 million 7-year contract with Paramount.

To escape the mob Tony Curtis and Jack Lemmon put on dresses in

SOME LIKE IT HOT

and join an all-girl band with Marilyn Monroe singing vocals.

Frank Capra Casts **Frank Sinatra** In *A Hole In The Head.*

ROD STEIGER'S AL CAPONE PRECIPITATES A RASH OF GANGSTER FILMS.

YUL BRYNNER (TOP) **Takes Over Role In** *Solomon and Sheba* **After The Untimely Death Of TYRONE POWER Last Year.**

Method Actor Marlon Brando Takes Over Directing Of *One-Eyed Jacks* After Director Stanley Kubrick Withdraws From The Film.

P A S S I N G S

Star of the renowned film **THE INFORMER**, for which he won an Oscar, actor Victor McLaglen, former wrestler, policeman and gold prospector, dies at age 72.

Charles Vidor, who directed **HANS CHRISTIAN ANDERSEN** and **A SONG TO REMEMBER** dies at age 58 of a heart attack in Vienna.

Theatre, movie, radio and television star Paul Douglas, whose performance in the long-running **BORN YESTERDAY** on Broadway brought him fame, dies of a heart attack at age 52.

Swashbuckling movie star Errol Flynn, whose adventures off-screen rivaled those he had in **ROBIN HOOD**, **ADVENTURES OF DON JUAN** and **CAPTAIN BLOOD**, dies at age 50.

One of the first and greatest movie moguls, producer, director and film pioneer Cecil B. DeMille, whose movies read like a greatest hits of the bible (**THE TEN COMMANDMENTS, SAMSON AND DELILAH, KING OF KINGS**), dies of a heart attack at age 77.

Best known for his Oscar winning role of Santa Claus in the classic **MIRACLE ON 34TH STREET**, actor Edmund Gwenn dies at age 81.

When your TV picture tube needs replacing, remember this...

NOW...AN RCA PICTURE TUBE TO FIT EVERY BUDGET!

All-New Premium

RCA Silverama.

Finest Picture Tube
Made Today!

Factory-Rebuilt

RCA Monogram

No Finer Rebuilt Picture
Tube Made!

Not just <u>one</u> RCA television picture tube...but a choice of <u>two</u>!

When the picture on your TV fades, dulls or blacks out—when your TV technician tells you the picture tube should be replaced, remember you now have a choice of two kinds of RCA picture tubes:

• **RCA SILVERAMA**—A premium picture tube—constructed of all-new glass and parts. Made for the TV viewer who wants the finest picture his set can deliver.

• **RCA MONOGRAM**—A rebuilt picture tube of dependable quality for the budget-minded. Reprocessed and tested in the same factory as RCA's premium picture tubes.

Both RCA SILVERAMA and RCA MONOGRAM are warranted for one full year...and there's a size to fit virtually every make and model TV set. Your local TV service technician can give you complete information and prices. Remember: for the best in television be sure to say...RCA.

RCA **RADIO CORPORATION OF AMERICA**

Electron Tube Division • Harrison, N. J.

What is a picture tube?

The picture tube — in simple terms — is actually a glass or metal bulb containing a "gun" which emits a stream of electrons. These electrons strike a layer of phosphor on the inside surface of the glass face — causing the phosphor to "glow", thus "painting" a TV picture on the face of the tube.

Two kinds of tubes

There are two kinds of picture tubes—new tubes constructed of all-new materials and parts, and also picture tubes known as "rebuilts". A "rebuilt" is simply a used picture tube that has been repaired by replacing the gun and possibly the phosphor and then reprocessed.

Actually, there's nothing wrong with "rebuilts". Retread tires and many other reconditioned devices can give you satisfactory performance. But the quality of most rebuilt products is limited by the rebuilder's skill and know-how. With a rebuilt picture tube the big question is—will it provide you with the bright, sharp picture you want for greater TV enjoyment? Now you *can* be sure! There is no finer rebuilt picture tube made than the RCA MONOGRAM.

So now you have a choice in RCA picture tubes:

• **RCA Silverama** . . . A premium picture tube—made of all-new glass and all-new parts.

• **RCA Monogram** . . . No finer factory-rebuilt picture tube made.

TELEVISION

The
MICKEY MOUSE
Club

goes off the air.

THE TWILIGHT ZONE

makes its television debut. Creator and host Rod Serling takes viewers into a new world called "The Sixth Dimension."

SO LONG FOR A WHILE

The long-running *Your Hit Parade* goes off the air.

CBS announces that **Edward R. Murrow** is taking a leave of absence for a year.

STEVE ALLEN

slaps a cease and desist warning on **Greyhound Bus Lines** from using the name **"Steverino"** for their dog after they terminate sponsorship of Allen's show.

Also Premiering
Five Fingers
Mr. Lucky
Peck's Bad Girl
Wichita Town
Pete Kelly's Blues

POPULAR

90% of American homes *have television sets, cutting into movie attendance.*

77 Sunset Strip
Adventures In Paradise
The Alaskans
Alcoa Presents
Alfred Hitchcock Presents
The Andy Williams Show
The Ann Sothern Show
Bachelor Father
Bat Masterson
The Betty Hutton Show
Black Saddle
Blondie
Bold Journey
Bold Venture
Bonanza
Bourbon Street Beat
Broken Arrow
Bronco
Buckskin
Californians
Cheyenne
Colt .45
Concentration
The Danny Thomas Show

The David Niven Show
December Bride
The Dennis O'Keefe Show
Dennis The Menace
The Deputy
The Dick Clark Show
The Donna Reed Show
Dragnet
The Ed Sullivan Show
Fibber McGee and Molly
Gunsmoke
Have Gun Will Travel
Hawaiian Eye
I Love Lucy
I've Got A Secret
The Invisible Man
The Jack Benny Show
The Jack Paar Show
The Jackie Gleason Show
The Jimmie Rodgers Show
John Gunther's High Road
The Joseph Cotten Show

Andy Williams

Alfred Hitchcock

Betty Hutton

Lucille Ball

PROGRAMS

A HORSE OF ANOTHER COLOR

Bonanza *is first western to be broadcast in color.*

Kraft Music Hall Presents: The Dave King Show

Laramie

Lassie

The Lawrence Welk Show

Leave It To Beaver

The Life And Legend Of Wyatt Earp

The Loretta Young Show

Love And Marriage

M Squad

Manhunt

The Many Loves Of Dobie Gillis

Maverick

Men Into Space

The Millionaire

Music For A Summer Night

Naked City

Name That Tune

Northwest Passage

Perry Mason

Peter Gunn

Jack Benny

Lassie

Phil Silvers

Walter Winchell

The Phil Silvers Show

Philip Marlowe

The Price Is Right

Rawhide

The Real McCoys

The Rebel

The Red Skelton Show

The Rifleman

Riverboat

Rocky And His Friends

The Rough Riders

Shirley Temple's Storybook

The Spike Jones Show

Startime

Steve Canyon

Tales Of Wells Fargo

The Thin Man

Tightrope

Trackdown

The Twilight Zone

The Untouchables

Wagon Train

The Walter Winchell Show

Wanted: Dead Or Alive

Westinghouse Desilu Playhouse

All This And Uncle Miltie Too

Euripides' Medea starring **Judith Anderson** kicks off New York's maverick WNTA-TV's new *"The Play Of The Week"* series followed by Ivan Turgenev's

A Month In The Country starring **Uta Hagen, Luther Adler** and **Alexander Scourby**.

Judith Anderson

Vivien Leigh makes her British television debut playing Sabrina in Thornton Wilder's The Skin Of Our Teeth.

16-year old beauty **Tuesday Weld** appears on CBS-TV's new teen television comedy THE MANY LOVES OF DOBIE GILLIS.

That's A Lot Of Velveeta

Singer **Perry Como** signs two-year, $25 million contract with Kraft Foods Company to produce 104 weekly one-hour shows with Como starring in a little less than half of them.

A viewing audience of eight million tune into NBC's production of **Gian-Carlo Menotti's** opera, Maria Golovin.

The television production of W. Somerset Maugham's The Moon And Sixpence garners **Sir Laurence Olivier** critical acclaim.

NBC's new team— **Chet Huntley** and **David Brinkley** garner awards for their in-depth news coverage and commentaries.

Emmy Awards

Series:

Dramatic: *Playhouse 90*

Comedy: *The Jack Benny Show*

Musical: *The Dinah Shore Chevy Show*

Western: *Maverick*

Performers:

Drama: Loretta Young
The Loretta Young Show

Raymond Burr
Perry Mason

Comedy: Jane Wyatt
Father Knows Best

Jack Benny
The Jack Benny Show

Fred Astaire's television special is nominated for, and wins, **nine Emmys** including **Actor, Program** and **Director.**

Famous Births

Jason **ALEXANDER**
Danny **BONADUCE**
Judd **NELSON**
Mackenzie **PHILLIPS**
David **HYDE PIERCE**
Jean **SMART**
Tracey **ULLMAN**

AND NOW FOR ALL YOU NUTS OUT THERE, AN INSTANT SOLUTION TO YOUR PROBLEMS

31-year old blonde psychologist **Joyce Brothers** gets late-night television psychiatry slot—*Consult Dr. Brothers*—following *The Jack Paar Show.*

The Peter Tchaikovsky Story,

presented by ***Walt Disney Presents*** is television's first stereophonic broadcast.

Americans see first newsreel film for television transmitted across the ocean by telephone cable—footage of Queen Mother and Princess Margaret waving goodbye to Queen Elizabeth as she leaves for Canada.

Yea, but can he sing country?

Clean cut crooner Columbia grad Pat Boone invests in two radio stations – one in Nashville and one in Fort Worth.

But Your Honor, Going Back To Dating Is Hell

In the first nationally televised murder trial, 45-year old divorcee, Mrs. Connie Nicholas, is tried and found guilty of manslaughter for the murder of her lover of 15 years, Forrest Teel, 54, executive Vice-President of Eli Lilly & Co., who left her for a younger woman.

The Federal Communications Commission opens hearings on television crime.

The "Equal Time" law is amended allowing coverage of political news and candidates without being obligated to give an equal amount of free time to other competing candidates.

PASSINGS

Beloved to several generations of youngsters, **Carl Switzer**, goofy Alfalfa on *Our Gang*, dies after a fight turns deadly at the age of 31.

George Reeves, who as television's super hero Superman could ward off any foe of disaster, shoots himself at age 45, several days before his intended marriage.

Lou Costello, who along with partner Bud Abbott, comprised one of the best-loved comedy teams in the history of show business dies several days before his 51st birthday. Among their many successes in theatre, radio, movies and television, their "Who's on First" skit remains one of the classic comic routines of all time.

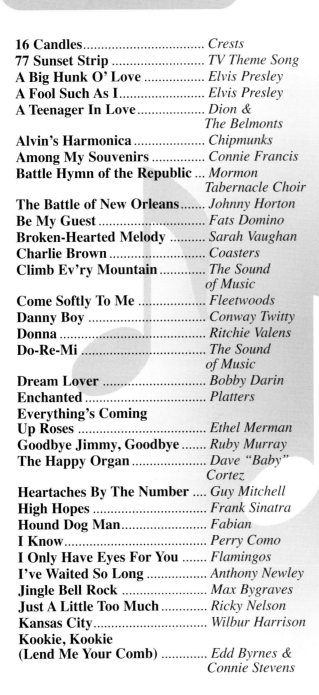

1959 POPULAR SONGS

MUSIC

16 Candles	Crests
77 Sunset Strip	TV Theme Song
A Big Hunk O' Love	Elvis Presley
A Fool Such As I	Elvis Presley
A Teenager In Love	Dion & The Belmonts
Alvin's Harmonica	Chipmunks
Among My Souvenirs	Connie Francis
Battle Hymn of the Republic	Mormon Tabernacle Choir
The Battle of New Orleans	Johnny Horton
Be My Guest	Fats Domino
Broken-Hearted Melody	Sarah Vaughan
Charlie Brown	Coasters
Climb Ev'ry Mountain	The Sound of Music
Come Softly To Me	Fleetwoods
Danny Boy	Conway Twitty
Donna	Ritchie Valens
Do-Re-Mi	The Sound of Music
Dream Lover	Bobby Darin
Enchanted	Platters
Everything's Coming Up Roses	Ethel Merman
Goodbye Jimmy, Goodbye	Ruby Murray
The Happy Organ	Dave "Baby" Cortez
Heartaches By The Number	Guy Mitchell
High Hopes	Frank Sinatra
Hound Dog Man	Fabian
I Know	Perry Como
I Only Have Eyes For You	Flamingos
I've Waited So Long	Anthony Newley
Jingle Bell Rock	Max Bygraves
Just A Little Too Much	Ricky Nelson
Kansas City	Wilbur Harrison
Kookie, Kookie (Lend Me Your Comb)	Edd Byrnes & Connie Stevens

Lipstick On Your Collar	Connie Francis
Lonely Boy	Paul Anka
Mack The Knife	Bobby Darin
Mr. Blue	Fleetwoods
My Happiness	Connie Francis
Never Be Anyone Else But You	Ricky Nelson
Only Sixteen	Craig Douglas
Peggy Sue Got Married	Buddy Holly
Personality	Lloyd Price
Peter Gunn Theme	Duane Eddy
Pillow Talk	Doris Day
Poison Ivy	Coasters
Put Your Head On My Shoulder	Paul Anka
Ragtime Cowboy Joe	Chipmunks
Sea of Love	Phil Phillips with the Twilights
Since I Don't Have You	Skyliners
Sixteen Going On Seventeen	The Sound of Music
Sleep Walk	Santo & Johnny
Smoke Gets In Your Eyes	Platters
Someone	Johnny Mathis
The Sound Of Music	Mary Martin
Stagger Lee	Lloyd Price
Sweeter Than You	Ricky Nelson
Take A Message To Mary	Everly Brothers
There Goes My Baby	Drifters
The Three Bells	Browns
Tijuana Jail	Kingston Trio
('Til) I Kissed You	Everly Brothers
Venus	Frankie Avalon
Way Down Yonder in New Orleans	Freddy Cannon
What A Difference A Day Makes	Dinah Washington
What'd I Say (Pt. 1)	Ray Charles
Why	Frankie Avalon

The newest sound in music...

General Electric Stereophonic Phonographs

Fashions by Anthony Blotta

RP1120

AS2

RP1160

AS4

Stereophonic Four-Speed Portable, RP1120 (shown above). Deluxe styling. Compatible Stereo/Monaural cartridge with sapphire-tipped dual styli. Plays conventional as well as stereo records, all sizes and speeds. Stereo jack. Twin 5¼-inch speakers. Loudness and tone controls. 45-rpm spindle. Cocoa and beige.

Amplifier/Speaker Unit (AS2) for complete stereophonic sound. Matched design and features. Pilot light.

Stereo-Musaphonic—True Fidelity Sound, RT1230 (shown at right). Stereo/Monaural cartridge—diamond and sapphire styli. 10-watt amplifier, external speaker terminals. Twin 8-inch speakers. Bass, treble, loudness controls. Tuner input jack, pilot light, 45-rpm spindle, matching hardwood legs. Hand-rubbed Mahogany or Blond Oak veneers.

Amplifier/Speaker Unit (AS15) for complete stereophonic sound. Matched design and features. Pilot light. 10-watt amplifier. Mahogany or Blond Oak veneers.

RT1230

AS15

Stereophonic Portable Phonograph with AM Radio, RP1160 (shown above). Stereo/Monaural cartridge with sapphire-tipped dual styli. 5.5-watt amplifier. Twin 6½-inch speakers. Continuous tone control; pull-push, on-off loudness control; pilot light; turntable compartment light and 45-rpm spindle. AM radio with illuminated slide-rule tuning dial. Two-tone gray.

Amplifier/Speaker Unit (AS4) for complete stereo. Matched design and features. Pilot light. 5.5 watts.

90-day warranty on parts and labor. Specifications subject to change. General Electric Company, Radio Receiver Department, Bridgeport 2, Connecticut.

Progress Is Our Most Important Product

GENERAL ⊕ ELECTRIC

With the biggest selling pop record in the U.S., **BOBBY DARIN'S** "Mack The Knife" catapults him into a headliner for the first time at the Sands Hotel in Las Vegas with his gross income for 1959 estimated at $250,000.

New Pop Recording Stars

ANNETTE FUNICELLO
BROOK BENTON
CHUBBY CHECKER
JAMES DARREN
FABIAN
ISLEY BROTHERS
JAN & DEAN*
CLIFF RICHARD
BOBBY RYDELL
BOBBY VEE

* Picked #1 New Group By Record Fans

BRITAIN GETS ITS FIRST TEEN IDOL— *Cliff Richard*

Folk rockers the KINGSTON TRIO sell more records than Fabian.

♪

"Puppy Love" is the first single recorded by 13-year old DOLLY PARTON.

♪

Her performance at the Newport Folk Festival wins recognition for JOAN BAEZ.

Headliners at the SANDS HOTEL, LAS VEGAS

Frank Sinatra	Dean Martin
Tony Bennett	Joey Bishop
Nat "King" Cole	Johnny Mathis
Sammy Davis, Jr.	Danny Thomas
Lena Horne	Louis Armstrong
Rowan & Martin	Bobby Darin

Bing's Boys

Estranged from their famous father, **Gary, Philip, Lindsay** and **Dennis Crosby** open their act at the Sahara Hotel in Las Vegas sans **Der Bingel** who is off on an Alaskan fishing trip.

Grammy Awards

Song Of The Year
The Battle Of New Orleans
Jimmy Driftwood, songwriter

Record Of The Year
Mack The Knife
Bobby Darin

Best New Artist
Bobby Darin

Best Male Vocal Performance
Come Dance With Me
Frank Sinatra

Best Female Vocal Performance
But Not For Me
Ella Fitzgerald

Best Performance By A Top 40 Artist
Midnight Flyer
Nat "King" Cole

Comedy Performance
Inside Shelley Berman
Shelley Berman

Spoken Word
A Lincoln Portrait
Carl Sandburg

RINGO GETS HIS FIRST BIG BANG

Ringo Starr joins
RORY STORM AND THE HURRICANES.

Neil Sedaka gives up his classical concert studies, switches to the world of rock 'n' roll and co-creates with Howard Greenfield "Oh! Carol" which hits the top ten.

MINE EYES HAVE SEEN THE TOP TEN ON THE CHARTS

"The Battle Hymn Of The Republic" recording by the Mormon Tabernacle Choir backed by the Philadelphia Symphony Orchestra, stuns the pop world by becoming a hit!

Having more than a few nips of the sauce before his recording session of "White Lightning," **George Jones** does 83 takes before it's a wrap.

DIRTY IS IN THE EAR OF THE LISTENER

Randy Wood, President of Dot Records, stops distribution of collaborative effort by Beat poet Jack Kerouac and jazz pianist Steve Allen calling the material on "Poetry Of The Beat Generation" in poor taste and not suitable for children.

Recovering after being beset with personal and professional problems, **Judy Garland** is booked by her husband, Sid Luft, to perform at the Metropolitan opera house for her official comeback where devoted fans will hear "Somewhere Over The Rainbow" and "The Trolley Song."

BREAKING INTO REAL ROCK

Actor/singer Pat Boone breaks his toe on a Hollywood set when he kicks what he thinks is a paper mache rock that turns out to be a stone.

PASSINGS

"Lady Day," beloved singer **Billie Holiday**, whose talent for singing jazz and blues was incomparable, dies at the age of 44. For her many fans throughout the world, she leaves behind such memorable record- ings as "STRANGE FRUIT," "FINE AND MELLOW" and "LOVER MAN."

Holly   *Richardson*   *Valens*

On tour in the Midwest with the Winter Dance Party, young rock 'n' roll stars **Buddy Holly**, **Ritchie Valens** and the "Big Bopper" **J.P. Richardson** are on their way from Iowa to North Dakota when their chartered plane crashes, killing everyone on board. All three had enjoyed hit songs, including Holly's "THAT'LL BE THE DAY," Valens' "LA BAMBA" and Richardson's "CHANTILLY LACE."

Saxophonist **Sidney Bechet**, legendary Storyville jazz musician who was even more famous abroad than in the U.S., dies in France at age 62.

Tenor sax player **Lester Young**, onetime member of Count Basie's band who also played with Billie Holiday and Benny Goodman, dies at age 9.

Writer of the classic song "FOR ME AND MY GAL," **George W. Meyer**, 75, dies in a Manhattan hotel fire.

"CHATTANOOGA CHOO-CHOO" lyricist **Mack Gordon** dies of a heart attack at age 54.

Creator of timeless songs "TAKE ME OUT TO THE BALL GAME" and "SHINE ON, HARVEST MOON," lyricist **Jack Norworth** dies at age 80.

Put Away Them Blue Suede Shoes And Take Out Those White Bucks

The faces of rock 'n' roll are changing. **Elvis Presley** is still in the Army, **Buddy Holly** and **Ritchie Valens** are dead, **Jerry Lee Lewis** is *persona non grata* because of his marriage to his underage cousin and **Chuck Berry** is also in trouble for bringing a minor across state lines. With these icons gone new, clean-cut faces begin to take over the pop music scene and we hear the music of **Pat Boone**, **James Darren**, **Frankie Avalon**, **Bobby Rydell**, **Fabian** and **Edd "Kookie" Byrnes** hit the radio airwaves.

♪ **Dick Clark's national tour of "Caravan of Stars," fueled by the success of his American Bandstand television show on ABC, brings in audiences in record numbers across the country.**

♪ **On the heels of a House sub-committee investigating payola in the music business, ABC forces Dick Clark to give up his interest in Swan Records when it is discovered that the rock 'n' roll recording of "Way Down Yonder" being plugged on American Bandstand was issued by... you guessed it... Swan Records.**

♪ **Rock 'n' roll idol Alan Freed's contract is terminated by WABC when he refuses to sign an affidavit that he took bribes from record companies.**

♪ **Famous Births:** Bryan Adams, Sheena Easton, Kathy Mattea, Marie Osmond, Richie Sambora, Randy Travis

jazz

Count Basie

Sonny Rollins

SONNY ROLLINS practices his tenor sax every day on New York's Williamsburg Bridge after he stops performing.

MILES DAVIS' "Buzzard Song" is a major hit.

ALL THAT JAZZ AND MORE
New York's Randall's Island is site of the world's biggest jam session featuring the great Dave Brubeck and his classical and traditional jazz fusion quartet dominating the event with "West Coast Jazz" trumpeter Miles Davis receiving accolades for his Miles Davis Sextet.

Paris resident American jazz singer **JOSEPHINE BAKER** comes out of retirement to star in new review **PARIS MES AMOURS** at the Olympia Music Hall.

The King Of Swing Is Swinging Again

After several slow years, the inimitable **Benny Goodman** is flying high again as he completes a triumphant European tour and opens his first nightclub appearance in two years at New York's famed Basin Street East.

Alan Lomax returns to the South to further research traditional American music and culture.

PASSING OUT THOSE GREEN NOTES

The Rockefeller Foundation makes a joint grant of $175,000 to Columbia and Princeton universities to be used to expand research and development in the field of electronic sounds.

PABLO CASALS

opens the third Casals Music Festival in San Juan, Puerto Rico.

Pulitzer Prize For Music

Concerto For Piano And Orchestra

John La Montaine

OPERA NEWS

Anyone Ever Hear Of Equal Pay?

Mezzo diva Risë Stevens cancels her 13-week contract at the San Francisco Opera Company after she learns Italian tenor Mario del Monaco is being paid more per performance.

•

A Colorado centennial production of Puccini's "The Girl Of The Golden West" is staged western style at Colorado's Red Rocks Theatre.

•

Metropolitan Opera House's production of Alban Berg's controversial atonal "Wozzeck" receives twenty-minute opening night ovation.

•

Swedish diva Birgit Nilsson makes victorious debut in Metropolitan Opera's production of "Tristan und Isolde."

•

A musical play based on Pirandello's "Six Characters in Search of an Author" is produced by the New York City Opera.

Lily Pons

Recovering from automobile acciden which put her in traction, coloratura soprano **Dolores Wilson** removes her neck brace and fills in for ailing **Lily Pons** who was to sing in "Lucia di Lammermoor" at the Met. Unfortunately, Miss Wilson finds herself back in the hospital in traction after suffering a collapse following her performance.

MARIA CALLAS and VAN CLIBURN pack the house at the Philadelphia Academy of Music where tickets are selling for up to $100 a pop.

Tempestuous diva MARIA CALLAS is furious when she learns young Australian soprano JOAN SUTHERLAND is hired by La Scala.

PASSINGS

38-year old opera singer **Mario Lanza** dies of a heart attack. The singer turned actor starred in "THE GREAT CARUSO" and will be remembered for his hit songs "LOVELIEST NIGHT OF THE YEAR" and "BE MY LOVE" each of which sold well over a million copies.

Composer **Heitor Villa-Lobos**, the most famous and respected Brazilian music man of his era, dies at age 75.

Classical Music

Leonard Bernstein and the New York Philharmonic receive unprecedented accolades by the tough Russian audiences after his reading of Shostakovich's "Fifth Symphony" calling it the best interpretation ever heard.

Under the auspices of the State Department **Leonard Bernstein** and the New York Philharmonic begin a 50-concert international tour covering 29 cities in 17 countries.

TURKISH DELIGHT
Music-hungry Turks crash through wooden police barricades at Istanbul's open-air theatre packing aisles and stairs to hear **Leonard Bernstein** conduct the 106-piece New York Philharmonic Orchestra.

Under the direction of **Leonard Bernstein**, the New York Philharmonic and the Dave Brubeck Quartet join together for *"Dialogues for Jazz Combo and Orchestra."*

As part of the cultural exchange program six Soviet musicians including Dmitri Shostakovich visit the U.S.

SHOSTAKOVICH

Dmitri Shostakovich breaks ranks with symphonic tradition and puts a Lindy Hop into his first opera called "Moskva, Cheromushki."

And then they wrote...

Second String Quartet
Elliott Carter

Symphony No. 7
David Diamond

A Hand of Bridge
Gian-Carlo Menotti & Samuel Barber

Concerto for Piano and Orchestra
Walter Piston

Variations for Violin and Orchestra
Wallingford Riegger

Three Moods
William Schuman

Conversations (concertino)
Gunther Schuller

Collected Poems
Virgil Thomson

Dance

- The New York City Ballet Does U.S. Premiere Of KURT WEILL'S "The Seven Deadly Sins."

- NOEL COWARD'S First Ballet, "London Morning" Falls On Its... Toes.

- JEROME ROBBINS' Ballets U.S.A. Receives Wide Acclaim During Its European Tour.

- DANCE HISTORY IS MADE When Martha Graham Joins Forces with George Balanchine And The New York City Ballet In A Production Called "Episodes."

Thanks to the remarkable efforts of impresario **SOL HUROK**, Moscow's Bolshoi Ballet arrives in New York for a 2-month tour of America and Canada and spends their first night at the circus at Madison Square Garden eating one of America's food favorites—the good old hot dog.

The Bolshoi's prima ballerina, 49-year old **GALINA ULANOVA** dazzled the who's who of communism with her work in *Giselle* at a 16-curtain call performance commemorating the 21st World Congress Of The Communist Party. The incomparable dancer appears on opening night at the Metropolitan Opera House in *Romeo and Juliet* winning highest critical acclaim for her work.

Royal Ballet prima ballerina **Margot Fonteyn** is detained by the Panamanian government on the suspicion of being involved in a plot to overthrow the government. Her husband, Roberto Arias, escapes being captured by jumping onto a passing shrimp boat.

In an effort to develop its own dancers, the Metropolitan Opera presents a performance of its resident ballet company for the first time.

Britain's oldest dance company, the Ballet Rambert, makes its American debut at Jacob's Pillow, Massachusetts.

Patricia Wilde and Jacques d'Amboise dance in Balanchine's "Native Dancers" inspired by a famous race horse.

Gagaku, the dancers of the Japanese Imperial household, make their American debut under the auspices of the New York City Ballet.

NEW YORK CITY'S LICENSE COMMISSIONER ORDERS THE FEMALE DANCERS OF LES BALLETS AFRICAINS TO COVER UP WHEN HE DISCOVERS THEY ARE NAKED FROM THE WAIST UP.

Zenith puts all its quality, its famous features, into new, slim portable-table TV

All-new—trim, Slim Classic design. Sets the style pace in portable TV. And only Zenith Portable TV has the handcrafted horizontal chassis to give you world-famous Zenith big-set performance. Sound-out-front speaker. The Zenith LaSalle, Model D1811C† in charcoal, $199.95.*

New slim, trim styling in a table model—blends with the decor of any room. Extra picture contrast from Zenith's Sunshine picture tube and Cinelens. Spotlight dial. The Zenith Gotham, Model D2317** in grained mahogany, walnut or blonde oak colors, $239.95*.

First time ever! Space Command® remote TV control in Zenith portable TV. Relax, don't get up. Tune TV from across the room with silent sound—no wires, no cords, no batteries.

Just touch a button on the control unit you hold in your hand—to change channels, turn set on and off, adjust volume, mute sound.

And only Zenith has it!

THE NEW LOOK IN TV IS THE SLIM CLASSIC LOOK! New, slim, trim Zenith portable-table TV fits beautifully, even in bookshelf space, in your living room, den, or bedroom.

See the world's most talked-about television at your Zenith dealer's!

ZENITH®
The quality goes in before the name goes on

ON BROADWAY

With Advance Sales In Excess Of Two Million Dollars, Rodgers & Hammerstein's THE SOUND OF MUSIC Opens To Rave Reviews And Is Called An Inescapable Crowd Pleaser.

ANOTHER OPENING, ANOTHER NIGHT

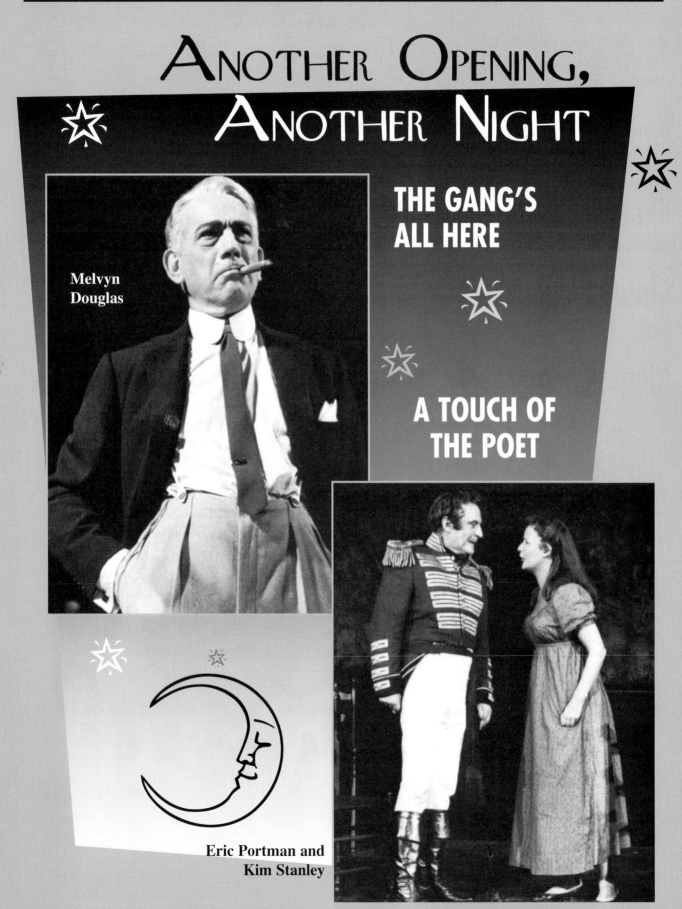

THE GANG'S ALL HERE

A TOUCH OF THE POET

Melvyn Douglas

Eric Portman and Kim Stanley

From left, Robert Coote, Rex Harrison and Julie Andrews

"My Fair Lady" Becomes My Rich Lady

"My Fair Lady" Celebrates Its Third Anniversary Surpassing $10,000,000 In Sales, Smashing Box Office Records On Four Continents.

Something To Beat The Drums About

Off-Broadway Musical Production Of "The Threepenny Opera" Celebrates Its History-Making Run With 1,405 Performances.

To Pay Or Not To Pay... That Is The Question

Joseph Papp Wins Battle With New York City Park Commissioner Robert Moses And Presents Free Shakespeare In The Park.

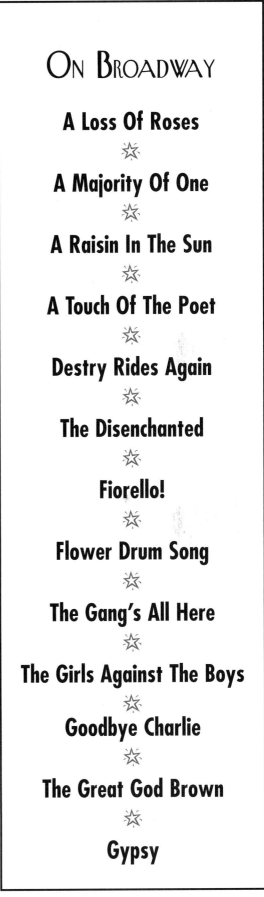

On Broadway

A Loss Of Roses

✫

A Majority Of One

✫

A Raisin In The Sun

✫

A Touch Of The Poet

✫

Destry Rides Again

✫

The Disenchanted

✫

Fiorello!

✫

Flower Drum Song

✫

The Gang's All Here

✫

The Girls Against The Boys

✫

Goodbye Charlie

✫

The Great God Brown

✫

Gypsy

The Stars At Night Are Bigger And Brighter

A London High School Is Dazzled By Cowboy Version Of "A Midsummer Night's Dream" Presented By An Acting Troupe From Howard Payne College Of Brownswood, Texas.

•

Second City Improvisational Troupe Begin Their Antics In Chicago.

•

After A Record 26-Year Run At The Theatre Mart In Los Angeles, "The Drunkard" Finally Closes.

•

Sir Laurence Olivier, Recognized As The Greatest Living Actor, Even Dazzled The Critics With His Brilliant Performance In Shakespeare's "Coriolanus" At The Stratford-On-Avon Production.

•

There's No Such Thing As A Small Part, Only A Small... Oh Well You Know The Rest

Academy Award Winner Shirley Booth Leaves Pulitzer Prize Winner William Inge's New Play "A Loss Of Roses" (Co-Starring Carol Haney And Warren Beatty) Before Its Broadway Opening On The Grounds That Her Part Is Not Important Enough.

Passings

Playwright **Maxwell Anderson**, whose work includes "What Price Glory" and "Bad Seed," as well as the Pulitzer Prize winning "Both Your Houses" dies at age 70.

Grand Dame of the theatre and member of the famed Drew-Barrymore thespians, **Ethel Barrymore**, who starred in only one film with her brothers John and Lionel, "Rasputin And The Empress," dies at age 79. Her supposed last words are "Is everybody happy... I know I'm happy."

Kay Kendall, actress in both theatre and film and wife of Rex Harrison, dies at age 33 of leukemia.

The Marriage-Go-Round

☆

The Miracle Worker

☆

Moonbirds

☆

Much Ado About Nothing

☆

My Fair Lady

☆

Once Upon A Mattress

☆

Only In America

☆

The Pleasure Of His Company

☆

Rashomon

☆

Requiem For A Nun

☆

The Sound Of Music

☆

Sweet Bird Of Youth

☆

West Side Story

Tony Awards
1959

OUTSTANDING PLAY

"J. B."

Archibald MacLeish

OUTSTANDING MUSICAL

"REDHEAD"

OUTSTANDING DRAMATIC ACTOR

JASON ROBARDS, JR.

"The Disenchanted"

OUTSTANDING DRAMATIC ACTRESS

GERTRUDE BERG

"A Majority Of One"

OUTSTANDING MUSICAL ACTOR

RICHARD KILEY

"Redhead"

OUTSTANDING MUSICAL ACTRESS

GWEN VERDON

"Redhead"

OUTSTANDING DIRECTOR

ELIA KAZAN

"J. B."

OUTSTANDING CHOREOGRAPHER

BOB FOSSE

"Redhead"

SPECIAL AWARDS

JOHN GIELGUD
For contributions to the theatre
and for his extraordinary insight
into the writings of Shakespeare
as demonstrated in his one-man
play "Ages of Man."

HOWARD LINDSAY and
RUSSELL CROUSE
For a collaboration that has
lasted longer than
Gilbert and Sullivan.

Drama Critics' Circle bypass Tennessee Williams' "Sweet Bird Of Youth" and Archibald MacLeish's "J. B." naming Lorraine Hansberry's "A Raisin In The Sun" Best American Play making her the first black writer to earn this coveted award.

AUCTIONS
Sotheby & Company, London

Peter Paul Rubens (record high price for a painting)
Adoration of the Magi — $ 770,000

El Greco
The Apostle James the Greater — 201,600

Pablo Picasso (record high for a painting by a living artist)
La Belle Hollandaise — 154,000

Paul Cezanne
Portrait of his wife — 112,000

Georges Braque
Femme a la Mandoline — 100,800

Thomas Gainsborough
Countess of Chesterfield — 95,200

Parke-Bernet Galleries, New York

Pierre August Renoir
Les Filles de Durand-Ruel — 255,000

Henri de Toulouse-Lautrec
Femme Rousse dans un Jardin — 180,000

PABLO PICASSO'S six bronze sculptures, "**Bathers**," are for sale at Manhattan's Fine Art Associates Gallery for $250,000

JASPER JOHNS' TARGET IS ACQUIRED BY THE MUSEUM OF MODERN ART, NY

Marie Antoinette's diamond necklace, along with baubles belonging to Queen Elizabeth and jeweler Harry Winston, help comprise "The Ageless Diamond" exhibition at Christie's in London. At Sotheby's, Winston purchases the "Westminster Tiara," 1,240 diamonds for $308,000.

WHO TOOK DA TUT?
In Cairo, museum officials announce the disappearance of King Tutankhamen's scepter.

Workmen in Athens uncover an ancient bronze of the god Apollo, and archaeologists attribute the work to the 6th century sculptor Antenor.

Salvador Dali informs
POPE JOHN XXIII of his desire to create a new church in Texas.

Marc Chagall is elected an Honorary Member of the American Academy of Arts and Letters. He is also named first artist-in-residence at Brandeis University in Massachusetts.

Starry, Starry Night
Planetariums open at the Boston Museum of Science and the Cleveland Natural History Museum.

Controversy rages in Los Angeles as the Building and Safety Department insists on conducting severe tests on the WATTS TOWERS to determine if the structures are sturdy enough to remain standing.

But It Speaks To Me
Swedish artist **Öyvind Fahlström** furiously removes one of his paintings from a Stockholm exhibit. Yes, the piece in question is his, but no, it isn't a painting. It is only packing to secure the pieces that he sent for the show.

Thousands watch as a 91-foot statue of Jesus Christ is dedicated in Portugal.

At the Carnegie International Exhibition in Pittsburgh, sculptor *Alexander Calder* wins first prize in sculpture.

The United States Exhibition in Moscow is seen by over 2 1/2 million Russians. Some artists represented include *Jackson Pollock, Robert Motherwell, Willem de Kooning, Mark Rothko* and *Andrew Wyeth.*

The first Paris Biennale exhibits over five hundred artists under 35 from forty-two countries.

Blind artists are the focus of a New York show, and their paintings, ceramics and sculpture are of such a high standard that it's impossible to tell they were created by people without sight.

Art owned by IBM, CBS, DeBeers and other businesses is on view at the "Art: USA: 59" presentation in New York.

PASSINGS

Dada Artist George Grosz, whose satirical portraits of German life invoked the ire of the Nazis, emigrated to the United States to avoid persecution. He returned to his hometown of Berlin only weeks before his death of a heart attack at age 65.

The Absolute Monarchist by Grosz

books

E.E. Cummings
100 POEMS

Allen Drury
ADVISE AND CONSENT

Margaret Mead
AN ANTHROPOLOGIST AT WORK

Mordecai Richler
THE APPRENTICESHIP OF
DUDDY KRAVITZ

Moss Hart
ACT ONE

Italo Calvino
THE BARON IN THE TREES

Robert St. John
BEN-GURION: THE BIOGRAPHY OF
AN EXTRAORDINARY MAN

Brendan Behan
THE BORSTAL BOY

Truman Capote
BREAKFAST AT TIFFANY'S

Frederic Sondern, Jr.
BROTHERHOOD OF EVIL: THE MAFIA

Joyce Cary
THE CAPTIVE AND THE FREE

Robert Penn Warren
THE CAVE

Aldous Huxley
COLLECTED ESSAYS

Pearl S. Buck
COMMAND THE MORNING

Sir Vivian Fuchs &
Sir Edmund Hillary
THE CROSSING OF ANTARCTICA

Salvador Dali
DALI ON MODERN ART

Taylor Caldwell
DEAR AND GLORIOUS PHYSICIAN

Jack Kerouac
DOCTOR SAX

June Havoc
EARLY HAVOC

Milton Berle & John Roeburt
EARTHQUAKE

William Strunk, Jr. & E.B. White
THE ELEMENTS OF STYLE

Richard Carrington
ELEPHANTS

Elspeth Huxley
THE FLAME TREES OF THIKA

C.G. Jung
FLYING SAUCERS: A MODERN MYTH
OF THINGS SEEN IN THE SKIES

Dr. DeForest Clinton Jarvis
FOLK MEDICINE

John O'Hara
FROM THE TERRACE

Harry Golden
FOR 2¢ PLAIN

Ian Fleming
GOLDFINGER

Philip Roth
GOODBYE, COLUMBUS
AND FIVE SHORT STORIES

Mae West
GOODNESS HAD NOTHING TO DO
WITH IT

Shirley Jackson
THE HAUNTING OF HILL HOUSE

James A. Michener
HAWAII

Saul Bellow
HENDERSON THE RAIN KING

Brendan Behan
THE HOSTAGE

Vladimir Nabokov
INVITATION TO A BEHEADING

Sacheverell Sitwell
JOURNEY TO THE ENDS OF TIME

Leonard Bernstein
THE JOY OF MUSIC

Romain Gary
LADY L

Boris Pasternak
THE LAST SUMMER

Evelyn Wood Reading Dynamics Institute opens in Washington.

Allen Ginsberg and **Gregory Corso** are two of the participants in a reading of Beat poets at Columbia University

Mystery writer **Raymond Chandler**, whose Philip Marlowe character remains the most popular detective in literature, dies at age 70. His books include "The Big Sleep," "Farewell, My Lovely" and "The Lady In The Lake."

Creator of the notorious Fu Manchu character, writer **Sax Rohmer** dies in London at or around age 75.

Duncan Hines, author of books that guide travelers to good places to stay and eat, dies at age 78.

Federal Judge Frederick Van Pelt Bryan rules that the U.S. Post Office ban on the unexpurgated American edition of D.H. Lawrence's "Lady Chatterley's Lover" is unconstitutional.

In Alabama, "The Rabbits' Wedding," a children's book about two married rabbits, is forced into the back rooms of libraries, available only by specific inquiry. The brouhaha is brought about because some lawmakers are convinced the married rabbits—one black, one white—are urging mixed marriages.

Aldous Huxley is the recipient of the American Academy of Arts and Letters Award of Merit medal. **Arthur Miller** receives the Gold Medal for drama.

Charles van Doren, ed.
LETTERS TO MOTHER: AN ANTHOLOGY

Grace Paley
THE LITTLE DISTURBANCES OF MAN

Ira Gershwin
LYRICS ON SEVERAL OCCASIONS

Jack Kerouac
MAGGIE CASSIDY

Richard Condon
THE MANCHURIAN CANDIDATE

William Faulkner
THE MANSION

Simone de Beauvoir
MEMOIRS OF A DUTIFUL DAUGHTER

William Gibson
THE MIRACLE WORKER

Laurie Lee
MOMENT OF WAR

Ira Wallace
MUSCLE BEACH

Jack Douglas
MY BROTHER WAS AN ONLY CHILD

Bertrand Russell
MY PHILOSOPHICAL DEVELOPMENT

Mary Astor
MY STORY: AN AUTOBIOGRAPHY

V.S. Naipaul
THE MYSTIC MASSEUR

William Burroughs
NAKED LUNCH

OBSERVATIONS
Photographs by Richard Avedon, Commentary by Truman Capote

Pablo Picasso
PICASSO DRAWINGS: FROM 1900 TO THE PRESENT

W. Somerset Maugham
POINTS OF VIEW

George D. Painter
PROUST: THE EARLY YEARS

Vladimir Nabokov
THE REAL LIFE OF SEBASTIAN KNIGHT

Grace Metalious
RETURN TO PEYTON PLACE

John Updike
THE SAME DOOR

Kurt Vonnegut
THE SIRENS OF TITAN

Arthur Koestler
THE SLEEPWALKERS

Robert A. Heinlein
STARSHIP TROOPERS

Colin Wilson
THE STATURE OF MAN

Vance Packard
THE STATUS SEEKERS

Fred Astaire
STEPS IN TIME

Peter De Vries
THE TENTS OF WICKEDNESS

Israel Cohen
THEODORE HERZL: FOUNDER OF POLITICAL ZIONISM

Herman Wouk
THIS IS MY GOD

Lillian Hellman
TOYS IN THE ATTIC

Thomas Griffith
WAIST-HIGH CULTURE

Samuel Beckett
WATT

Bertrand Russell
WISDOM OF THE WEST

James Thurber
THE YEARS WITH ROSS

PRIZES

NOBEL

Literature:
SALVATORE QUASIMODO, *ITALY*

PULITZER

Fiction:
ROBERT LEWIS TAYLOR
THE TRAVELS OF JAIMIE MCPHEETERS

Poetry:
STANLEY KUNITZ
SELECTED POEMS 1928-1958

History:
LEONARD D. WHITE & JEAN SCHNEIDER
THE REPUBLICAN ERA: 1869-1901

Journalism:
UTICA OBSERVER-DISPATCH & THE UTICA DAILY PRESS

National Reporting:
HOWARD VAN SMITH
MIAMI NEWS

International Reporting:
JOSEPH MARTIN & PHILIP SANTORA
THE NEW YORK DAILY NEWS

Editorial Cartooning:
BILL MAULDIN
ST. LOUIS POST-DISPATCH

Biography or Autobiography:
ARTHUR WALWORTH
WOODROW WILSON: AMERICAN PROPHET

A 15th-Century Manuscript Of **Chaucer's Canterbury Tales,** Complete With Correction Marks, **Sells For $42,560** In London.

A Letter Written By **Martha Washington** In 1799 **Sells For $1,400** At A New York Auction.

$11,750 buys a three bedroom, two bathroom house with a swimming pool near Phoenix, Arizona. Down payment is approximately **$400**.

Nearly 50,000 pools are built in backyards across the country, many for middle-class families.

Key words in home furnishings include

walnut
grace
modern
affordable
traditional
shelves
pattern
skylights
vinyl
wallpaper
lengthy

Brown, blue, green, orange and **yellow** are some of the year's favorite decorating colors.

Construction for the first completely automated post office in the U.S. begins in Providence, Rhode Island.

A gigantic aluminum frame structure named "Octet Truss," designed by **R. Buckminster Fuller**, can be seen in New York at the Museum of Modern Art.

R. Buckminster Fuller's gold geodesic dome houses the entire United States Exhibition in Moscow.

Designer Charles Eames produces a documentary for the United States Exhibition which shows the Russian people different aspects of life in America.

Ground is broken in London for what is to be the highest office building in Great Britain.

Looking like an enormous martini glass, a water tower is built in Helsinki, Finland.

FRANCE

Imminent destruction of a Le Corbusier designed home outside of Paris causes an outcry from architects around the world.

•

An underground church is built in Lourdes.

•

Le Corbusier finishes Convent La Tourette near Lyons.

architecture + design

Models of well-known buildings can be seen when "Form Givers At Mid-Century" opens at the Corcoran Gallery in Washington D.C. Represented architects include Frank Lloyd Wright, Eero Saarinen, Ludwig Mies van der Rohe, and Le Corbusier.

Harvard's Walter Gropius receives the American Institute of Architects' gold medal.

Winners of the American Institute of Architects' Honor Awards include I.M. Pei & Associates and Eero Saarinen & Associates.

San Francisco's Crown Zellerbach and John Hancock buildings, designed by famed architectural firm **Skidmore, Owings & Merrill** are completed, beginning the revitalization of the Market Street area.

It's A Wright, Wright, Wright World

Despite his death on April 9th, numerous **FRANK LLOYD WRIGHT** projects garner attention throughout the year.

OCTOBER SEES THE GRAND OPENING of the ultra-modern, cylindrical Solomon R. Guggenheim Museum *(above)*, the only Wright structure in Manhattan. It is by far the grandest gallery for non-objective art in the world.

HIS BETH SHALOM SYNAGOGUE in Elkins Park, Pennsylvania, opens.

PATTERNED FABRICS for home use designed by Wright are available.

PASSINGS

Architect's architect **FRANK LLOYD WRIGHT**, whose designs revolutionized the architecture field and who incorporated the surrounding natural elements into his designs, is dead at age 89. Famous throughout the world, his structures dot landscapes as far away as Tokyo and as close as his own home, "Taliesin," in Wisconsin.

Fems
FEMININE NAPKINS

Now! A longer napkin you can wear and forget!

Shop, work, play as you please.

At long last here's a feminine napkin you can wear and forget!

Fems feminine napkins are longer to fit better and absorb better. Yet, there's not an ounce of extra bulk.

Now your protection stays put even under stress, thanks to the extra length of the tab ends. What a feeling of security!

Forget about stains. Wear your best party dress, knowing there's a protective safety-cushion to prevent accidents, whether you're seated or moving about.

Forget about shifting and binding. Longer Fems feminine napkins are made to adjust to your body without discomfort—no matter how active you may be.

Forget about chafing. Touch the chafe-free covering to the inside of your wrist, where your skin is extra sensitive. No wonder Fems bring welcome relief from chafing.

Fems absorb quickly. That's another protection against chafing. And both the covering and inner materials are designed to keep surfaces comfortably dry, even during the heaviest flow.

Would you pay a few cents more for all this comfort and confidence? Of course you would!

Next time wear Fems—and forget!

FEMS is a trademark of Kimberly-Clark Corp.

In The News

furs by Revillon

E WALDORF-ASTORIA

Wherever automobiles are seen and appreciated, the Cadillac name has, over the years, become an accepted synonym for "quality". Yet never before has the Cadillac car represented such a *high* standard of excellence as it does today. In its great beauty and majesty . . . in its fineness of performance . . . in the elegance of its Fleetwood interiors . . . and in the skill of its craftsmanship . . . it is far and away the finest fruit of Cadillac's unending quest for quality. We believe that a personal inspection will convince you of this fact—and that an hour at the wheel will add certainty to conviction. Why not accept your dealer's invitation to visit him soon—for a ride and a revelation?

CADILLAC MOTOR CAR DIVISION • GENERAL MOTORS CORPORATION
EVERY WINDOW OF EVERY CADILLAC IS SAFETY PLATE GLASS

Cadillac ...world's best synonym for quality!

Politics and World Events

Vice-President Richard Nixon *(right)* is accompanied by Soviet Premier Nikita Khrushchev *(far left)* on his visit to the United States Exhibition in Moscow.

Nixon's free-swinging kitchen debate sets the stage for Mr. K's tour of the United States. Later, Mr. Nixon meets privately for 5 ½ hours with the Soviet Prime Minister at his country home outside of Moscow.

Khrushchev is greeted in Washington, D.C. by President Eisenhower.

For a whirlwind two weeks, Khrushchev and his moods dominated the news leaving no doubt as to his toughness and his faith in the future of communism.

The Berlin crisis Khrushchev provoked fades when he and President Eisenhower meet for summit talks at Camp David.

Relations with the Soviets and the free world take on a more amiable tone after the talks at Camp David but the underlying realities were unchanged — notably the Soviet drive to match American technology.

AT TALKS BEING HELD IN GENEVA, THE UNITED STATES AND GREAT BRITAIN OFFER THE SOVIETS GUARANTEES FOR IMPARTIAL INTERNATIONAL CONTROL OF TEST BAN.

THE SOVIETS CLAIM GREATER POWER IN VIEW OF THEIR ROCKET SUCCESS.

TWO SOVIET MIG JET FIGHTERS ATTACK NAVY PATROL PLANE OVER SEA OF JAPAN ACCORDING TO U.S. DEFENSE DEPARTMENT.

APPEARING ON RUSSIAN TELEVISION, VICE-PRESIDENT RICHARD NIXON ASSERTS END OF FEAR DEPENDS ON SOVIET POLICIES.

SOVIET PREMIER KHRUSHCHEV RETURNS TO MOSCOW AFTER SUCCESSFUL TALKS WITH PRESIDENT EISENHOWER WHERE THEY REPORTED TO HAVE REACHED UNDERSTANDINGS THAT WOULD RELIEVE WORLD TENSION.

SOVIETS REFUSE NIXON VISIT TO MISSILE PLANT.

Nikita Khrushchev

Soviets Sign Pact With Peking
To Aid In Chinese Industrial Expansion.

Leningrad

Moscow

Kiev

U.S.S.R.

U.S.S.R. And East Germany Sign 6-Year Trade Treaty
Claiming It To Be The Biggest In History.

Khrushchev Presides Over Newly-Formed Hungarian Party Congress.

Western Plan For Big Four Parley On Germany Rejected By The Soviets.

In The First Visit By A British Prime Minister Since Curchill's During Wwii, Harold Macmillan Spends Ten-Days In The Soviet Union. He And Khrushchev Meet To Speak Of "Cultural Matters Of Interest Between The Two Countries."

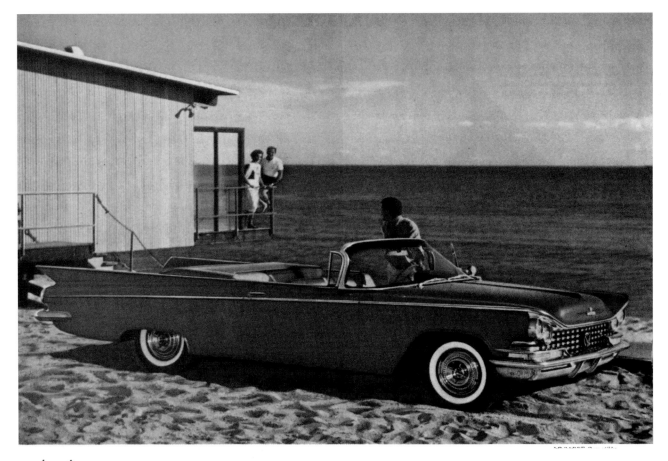

*Whatever car you have in mind . . .
you're better off with a Buick!*

Almost any new American car you're thinking of buying falls within reach of today's Buick price range.

And when this same money pays for a Buick, today more than ever before it brings you things you just can't buy elsewhere!

It pays for a very special feeling of wisdom and pride. It pays for the magic in the Buick name itself—a sense of quality, tradition, reliability. And it pays—in ways you can touch and feel—for the most exciting beauty, the most advanced and expert performance ever built into Buick cars.

If you're thinking of buying a car, don't fail to see your Quality Buick Dealer. He has some wonderful new surprises for your money.

New Magic-Mirror finishes • New super-quiet Bodies by Fisher • Safety PLATE Glass all around • New Equipoise ride • New fin-cooled brakes, front and rear • Aluminum front brake drums • Thriftier, higher compression, more powerful Wildcat engines • New electric windshield wipers • New Buick Easy Power Steering* • Exclusive Twin-Turbine and Triple-Turbine transmissions* • New Automatic heat and fresh air control*.

(*Optional at extra cost on certain models.)

LⁱSABRE *The thriftiest Buick*   **INVICTA** *The most spirited Buick*   **ELECTRA** *The most luxurious Buick*

BUICK MOTOR DIVISION, GENERAL MOTORS CORPORATION

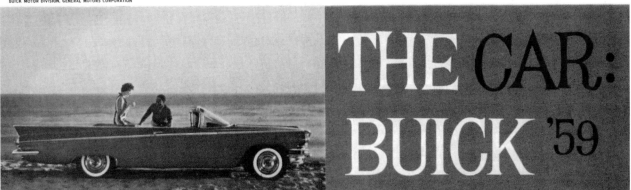

THE CAR:
BUICK '59

Cuban Rebel Leader FIDEL CASTRO

Overthrows The **Fulgencio Batista Government** Replacing Him With **Manuel Urrutia** As Provisional President. **Batista** Flees Cuba.

- Castro Named Head Of Cuban Army.
- Fidel Castro Sworn In As Cuban Premier.

Former Argentine Physician, **Ernesto "Che" Guevara,** Is Appointed President Of The National Bank Of Cuba.

Fidel Castro

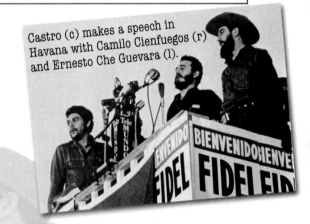

Castro (c) makes a speech in Havana with Camilo Cienfuegos (r) and Ernesto Che Guevara (l).

Over 4,500 People Arrested In Cuba As The Castro Government Launches Counter-Offensive Against Anti-Castro Elements.

Due To "Moral Differences" With Cuba's President Urrutia, Castro Resigns As Premier But Cabinet Refuses To Accept Resignation.

Five Cuban Cabinet Ministers Resign In Protest Over Castro's Agrarian Reform Bill Which Calls For The Confiscation Of Thousands Of Acres Of Cuban And Foreign-Owned Property.

Cuban Government Seizes Control Of U.S.-Owned Cuban Telephone Company.

Cuba Severs Diplomatic Relations With Dominican Republic.

Castro Eligible For Presidency As Electoral Age Is Reduced To 30.

Cuban Exiles Arrested In U.S. After They're Caught Loading Bombs On A Cuban-Bound Plane.

New Cuban Government Receives U.S. Recognition.

Castro Accuses U.S. Of Bombing Havana.

U.S. Accuses Cuba Of Jeopardizing Relations.

Castro Refuses To Pledge Support To U.S. In Cold War Against Soviets.

U.S. opposes sale of British jets to Cuba.

During His U.S. Visit, Cuban Premier Fidel Castro Denies Being A Communist In Speech Given To The American Society Of Newspaper Editors.

Castro and his troops are welcomed by a wildly jubilant crowd following his incredible victory over Batista.

Through the months that follow, the leftist course of his social reforms rouse new opposition. Discontent spreads through the Caribbean and Castro lashes out at his critics with court-martials at home and furious denunciation of U.S. policies. At year's end, Cuba remains a scene of unrest.

Boy denounces Batista supporter.

61

LAOS

Laos, a strategic key to Southeast Asia's richest area, is attacked by guerilla forces from communist Vietnam, a Chinese puppet state.

China's mobilization and aggressiveness cause mounting concern.

Leading Theoretician Liu Shao-chi Is Elected Chairman By China's National People's Congress, Succeeding **Mao Tse-tung** Who Remains Head Of The Communist Party.

Nikita Khrushchev Arrives In Peking To Observe A Huge Display Of Military Might Commemorating Communist China's Tenth Anniversary.

Mao Tse-tung

Asia

Mongolia

☆Ulaan Baatar

Japan ☆Tokyo

Peking ☆

Seoul ☆

Korea

China

Shanghai ☆

Japanese Demonstrators Protest Signing Of Sino-American Defense Treaty.

Tibet

Nepal

India

☆Calcutta

Burma

☆Hanoi

Laos

Vietnam

Philippines

☆Bombay

Thailand

Manila ☆

Rangoon ☆

Cambodia

Bangkok ☆

Phnom Penh ☆ ☆Saigon

Ceylon

☆Singapore

Communist China Barred Entry To U.N. For 9th Consecutive Year.

Ex-Emperor Of China And Japanese Puppet State Manchukuo, **Henry Pu Yi**, Receives Pardon From Communist China.

Readying Supply Lines On The Ho Chi Minh Trail, Hanoi Takes Control Of The Growing Communist Rebellion In South Vietnam.

In Preparation For Attack, North Vietnam Troops Join Forces With The Pathet Lao In Laos. Ike Steps Up Financial Aid To Laotian Government.

Singapore Gets Self-Rule And Holds First Elections.

King Mahendra Opens Nepal's First Elected Parliament.

PLEASE... <u>PLEASE</u> LET US GET IN A WORD ABOUT THIS

fresh, clean taste!

Copyright 1959 by The Seven-Up Company

Nothing does it like Seven-Up

...we won't take a minute...just have to point out...most popular invention next to the telephone is 7-Up... sparkles like crazy...tastes too fresh and clean for words...even leaves your mouth feeling fresh and clean when you finish the bottle! YOU ALREADY KNOW? Pardon us! "FRESH UP" WITH SEVEN-UP

Tibet

🏵 **CELEBRATION OF THE TIBETAN NEW YEAR** Turns Into Bloody Fighting in Lhasa As The Chinese Move To Arrest The Dalai Lama, Who Is Rumored To Have Fled To India. Following The Death Of 2,000 Troops, Chinese Reinforcements Stop The Rebellion.

🏵 **CHINESE PREMIER CHOU EN-LAI** Claims Dalai Lama Victim Of Indian Kidnapping.

🏵 **DALAI LAMA ASKS UNITED NATIONS** For Intervention Against Chinese Occupation Of Tibet.

🏵 **PANCHEN LAMA IS APPOINTED NEW RULER OF TIBET** As Communist China Dissolves The Tibetan Local Government Of The Dalai Lama.

🏵 **THE DALAI LAMA WILL LIVE IN MUSSOORIE,** According To An Announcement Made By The Indian Foreign Ministry.

India

🏵 **INDIAN PRIME MINISTER NEHRU** Accuses Communist China Of Violating Trade And Travel Agreement Between India And Tibet.

🏵 **INDIAN PRIME MINISTER NEHRU CRITICIZES INDIAN COMMUNISTS** For Supporting Communist China's Suppression Of Tibetan Revolt.

🏵 **INDIA DISPATCHES SOLDIERS** To Tibet Border To Prevent Chinese Advance Into India.

🏵 **INDIAN PRIME MINISTER JAWAHARLAL NEHRU'S ONLY DAUGHTER,** Indira Gandhi, Is Elected President Of The Congress Party.

Jawaharlal Nehru

Dalai Lama

President Eisenhower

returns to Washington after his historic 11-nation tour spanning three continents where he delivers his American message of *"peace and friendship in freedom."*

Ike receives a tumultuous welcome on his arrival in Paris.

Following Alaska, And After Petitioning 17 Times For Statehood, President Eisenhower Proclaims A Jubilant Hawaii The 50th State Of The Union.

Ike Signs Bill Making Alaska The 49th State. New Flag With Seven Rows Of Seven Stars To Become Official July 4th.

President Eisenhower Submits To Congress Special 7-Point Civil Rights Program Including Support And Encouragement For School Integration.

President Eisenhower Tells Congress He Will Send Nuclear Arms To Greece.

Federal Debt Ceiling Raised To $295 Billion By President Eisenhower.

U.S. Congress Urged By Ike To Approve His Program For Economic, Military And Technical Aid To Foreign Nations Next Year.

Senator Humbert H. Humphrey Throws Hat Into Bid For Democratic Presidential Nomination Along With Senators Stuart Symington Of Missouri, John F. Kennedy Of Massachusetts And Majority Leader Lyndon B. Johnson.

Former Atomic Energy Chairman, Lewis L. Strauss, Denied Confirmation As Secretary Of Commerce – The First Cabinet Rejection In 34 Years.

Potter Stewart Confirmed As Associate Justice Of The Supreme Court.

Vice President Richard Nixon Named Chairman Of Permanent Cabinet Committee On Price Stability For Economic Growth.

At The Urging Of Her Husband, Henry R. Luce, Editor-in-Chief Of Time, Life And Fortune, Newly Appointed Ambassador To Brazil, Clare Boothe Luce, Resigns As A Result Of Attacks On Her By Senator Wayne Morse Who Called Her "Unqualified" And "Emotionally Unstable," Stating That He Had Destroyed The Climate Of Goodwill Necessary For Making Her Work Successful.

For The First Time In 26 Years A Democrat – Gaylord A. Nelson – Takes Office As Governor Of Wisconsin.

Senator John F. Kennedy Proposes Labor Bill Aimed At Driving Out Racketeers.

Texas Senator, Lyndon Johnson, Throws All His Support Behind The Passage Of The Civil Rights Bill.

Nixon in Poland

Despite lack of notice in the press of the Vice-President's schedule, 25,000 Poles line the streets to offer a most enthusiastic welcome.

The turnout overshadows by far Poland's recent reception given for Soviet Premier Nikita Khrushchev which seems to indicate the popular temper in what is comparatively the freest of the iron curtain countries. The demands on the Vice-President's talents in tact and diplomacy are possibly the greatest of his entire tour.

On their return to the United States, the Nixons are greeted warmly by a crowd of nearly 4,000 people including most of the White House staff as well as just about every Republican congressman and senator.

The Vice-President's remarks appear to be non-partisan: *"The people of the Soviet Union, and even more the people of Poland, who lost one out of four citizens in World War II, have suffered a great deal in wartime and they desperately want peace."*

IRELAND'S PRIME MINISTER
EAMON DE VALERA Resigns Post In Order To Run For The Presidency.

EAMON DE VALERA ELECTED PRESIDENT OF IRELAND. Sean Lemass
Takes Over As Prime Minister.

JOHN D. PROFUMO Appointed Britain's Minister Of State, Foreign Office.

TO SPUR ECONOMIC GROWTH, Britain
Passes $1 Billion Tax Cut.

ENGLAND'S HOUSE OF COMMONS Sees Double Majority
Under Macmillan's Leadership.

CHARLES DE GAULLE Is
Sworn In As President Of The Fifth Republic At Inaugural Ceremony Held At The Élysée Palace In Paris And Now Wields More Power Than Any French Leader Since Emperor Napoleon III.

Western Europe

Norway
Sweden
Finland
☆ Oslo
☆ Helsinki
☆ Stockholm
United Kingdom
☆ Edinburgh
Denmark
☆ Copenhagen
Dublin ☆
☆ London
☆ Amsterdam
Holland
Belgium
☆ Berlin
Poland
☆ Warsaw
Brussels ☆
Luxembourg
☆ Prague
Paris ☆
Germany
Czechoslovakia
France
☆ Zurich
☆ Vienna
Switzerland
Austria
☆ Budapest
Hungary
Portugal
☆ Madrid
Spain
Italy
Yugoslavia
☆ Belgrade
☆ Rome
Albania
Greece
☆ Athens

ASSASSINATION ATTEMPT Made Against France's **Francois Mitterrand**.

SPAIN BECOMES 18th MEMBER
Of Organization For European Economic Cooperation.

SPECIAL ELECTORAL COLLEGE Elects **Heinrich Luebke**
President Of West Germany.

PRESIDENT EISENHOWER RECEIVES WARM WELCOME
By West Germans Who Yell *"We Stand By Your Side."*

Citing "Continuously Hostile Attitude" Of The 18-Member National Council, Monaco's **Prince Rainier III** Suspends The 1911 Constitution Appointing An Eight-Member Council To Help Him Administer The Principality.

Africa

✴ Charged With Inciting Violence, Belgian Congo's PATRICE LUMUMBA Is Arrested After Troops Fire On Mobs Rioting For Independence.

✴ Civil War Impedes Plans For Congo Independence.

✴ U.S. Troops To Leave Morocco By 1963 According To An Announcement Made Jointly By PRESIDENT EISENHOWER And KING MOHAMMED.

ARCHBISHOP MAKARIOS RETURNS TO CYPRUS AFTER THREE-YEAR EXILE.

MAKARIOS

EXILED BY THE BRITISH IN 1956, **ARCHBISHOP MAKARIOS** BEATS HIS TURKISH CYPRIOT OPPONENT BECOMING NEW LEADER OF GREECE.

✴ French PRESIDENT DE GAULLE To Offer Algeria Elected Government.

✴ PRESIDENT DE GAULLE'S Speech On Algerian Independence Results In Walk-Out Of Nine Gaullist Deputies.

✴ Under PRIME MINISTER HENDRIK VERWOERD'S Government, South Africa Passes A "Bantustan" Bill Removing All Coloreds From The Common Electoral Roll And Voting Age Is Reduced To 18 To Increase The Number Of White Votes Deepening Apartheid.

Middle East

Jordan's King Hussein Vows End Of Feud With Egypt's President Nasser.

☪ Iran Accepts U.S. Proposal For Aid Rejecting Soviet Offer.

☪ Iran Renounces Pact Made With Soviet Union In 1921.

☪ Continued Aid Pledged To Iran, Pakistan And Turkey By U.S.

☪ Syria Reports Iraqi Air Attack.

☪ Following The Revolution, Iraq Pulls Out Of Baghdad Pact.

☪ A New Constitution Fashioned After The U.S. Constitution Is Signed By President Habib Bourguiba Of Tunisia.

☪ Diplomatic Relations Reopen Between Jordan And United Arab Republic.

☪ Central Treaty Organization (CENTO) Holds First Meeting With Baghdad Pact Ministers Under New Name.

☪ Egypt And The Sudan End 30-Year Rivalry Agreeing To Share The Waters Of Nile River – Paves Way For Construction Of Aswan Dam.

☪ Iraqi Premier Kassem Wounded In Assassination Attempt.

Gamal A. Nasser

Nasser Arrests 200 Communists.

✡ Shimon Peres Becomes Israel's Deputy Minister Of Defense.

✡ Arab League Council Warns Hungary, Poland And Rumania That Jewish Emigration To Israel Is Supporting Aggression On Arab States.

✡ Addressing The United Nations, Israeli Foreign Minister Golda Meir Denounces the United Arab Republic For Barring Israeli Ships From Suez Canal.

✡ Under Ben Gurion's Leadership, Israel's Mapai Party Gains In Legislative Elections.

Golda Meir   David Ben Gurion

73

NATO TO LOSE French Mediterranean Support In Case Of War.

NEWLY-FORMED

International Development Association Approved By 68 World Bank Nations.

AUSTRIA, BRITAIN, DENMARK, NORWAY, PORTUGAL, SWEDEN AND SWITZERLAND,

Europe's Outer Seven Nations, Form Free Trade Region.

U. N. GENERAL ASSEMBLY

Adopts East-West Resolution To Establish U. N. Committee On The Peaceful Uses Of Outer Space.

FRANCE ASKED BY U. N.

Not To Make Nuclear Bombs.

President Of Haiti Francois Duvalier Announces Suspension Of Dictatorial Powers.

Romulo Betancourt Sworn In As Constitutional President Of Venezuela.

U.S. Troops Called In To Quell Riots Over American Control Of Panama Canal Zone.

PEOPLE

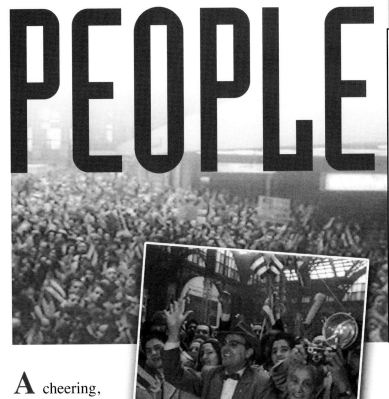

Fidel Castro

receives a tumultuous welcome in New York City in one of the most enthusiastic receptions for a visiting notable in quite a while.

A cheering, singing, flag-waving crowd of thousands gather to greet the Cuban revolutionary leader and premier.

Outside Penn Station, police break up a demonstration of supporters of ousted dictator Batista.

A heavily guarded Castro makes his way past the security guards to greet the crowd despite rumors of assassination plots against him.

Almost swamped by the excited crowd, it takes Castro a record 24 minutes to cross the street to his hotel.

Budweiser®

Where there's Life...there's Bud®

HARMONY. Right on the label you'll find a list of the ingredients that blend together to make Budweiser the masterpiece it is...the King of Beers.

ANHEUSER-BUSCH, INC. · ST. LOUIS · NEWARK · LOS ANGELES · MIAMI

Quiz Show Scandal

In the Senate hearing room,
the dramatic climax of the probe of fixed and rigged quiz shows is taking place.

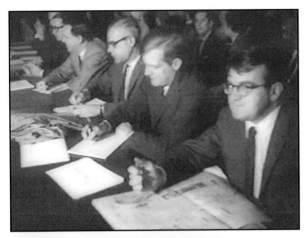

Charles' wife and father, poet Mark Van Doren, are among the spectators.

Committee chairman, Senator Orin Harris *(left)*, opens the hearing as Charles Van Doren *(right)* arrives to apologize and explain to the millions of fans whose friendship and respect he had won.

In his quiz show appearances, Van Doren won $129,000 and earned a handsome broadcasting contract. Van Doren retracts his earlier denials of getting any assistance and admits he received dramatic coaching, the questions and many of the answers.

His statement is a rueful and moving real-ization that for his wealth and fame he paid a bitterly high price.

After a 10-year absence from Hollywood, **INGRID BERGMAN** returns to host the Academy Awards ceremony. Bergman and her former husband, director **ROBERTO ROSSELLINI**, are ordered to appear in a Roman court when Rossellini refuses to return his three children to Bergman after they vacationed with him in Italy. Bergman wins the custody battle in a Paris courtroom.

★ Actress **DIANE VARSI** Gives Up Promising Hollywood Career And Goes Into Seclusion In Bennington, Vermont Stating That Acting Is Detrimental To Her Well Being.

★ Suffering From Nervous Fatigue, Hollywood's Beautiful **LINDA DARNELL** Is Hypnotized To Help Her Memorize The Lines For Her Role In The Play "Late Love" Opening In Chicago And Receives Wonderful Reviews.

★ Spending Almost Nine Months At The Menninger Clinic Recovering From A Nervous Breakdown, Hollywood Star **GENE TIERNEY** Works As A Sales Lady In A Small Ladies Apparel Shop In Topeka, Kansas.

PLEASE DON'T PICK THE FLOWERS

During a party at Rio de Janeiro's Copacabana Hotel, much to the joy of the assembled press corp., **JAYNE MANSFIELD** loses the top of her dress baring her heavily endowed 40-21-36 figure after overly enthusiastic Brazilian fans pick the strategically placed roses attached to her dress. Her Mr. Universe husband, Mickey Hargitay, saves the day by wrapping Jayne in his coat.

Mansfield

Elizabeth Taylor

Converts To Judaism, The Religion Of Her Late Husband, Mike Todd And The Religion Of Her Soon-To-Be-Husband, Eddie Fisher.

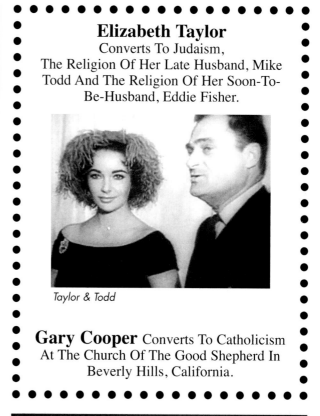

Taylor & Todd

Gary Cooper Converts To Catholicism At The Church Of The Good Shepherd In Beverly Hills, California.

TO ALEC, WITH LOVE
Having Won An Oscar For His Brilliant Performance In *THE BRIDGE ON THE RIVER KWAI*, **ALEC GUINNESS** Hits Queen Elizabeth's List Of Honorees Becoming A Knight Bachelor - Heretofore To Be Known As Sir Alec.
JUDITH ANDERSON Is Made British Dame

UP WITH THE NECKLINES GIRLS!

Sex kittens **BRIGITTE BARDOT** and **KIM NOVAK** vow to give up sexy, "bitchy" parts in exchange for more serious roles.

Bardot

EVERYBODY'S BABE

Much to the chagrin of new French army recruit, Jacques Charrier, when he reports to his assigned barracks, he finds a pinup picture of his beautiful wife, **BRIGITTE BARDOT**, hanging over nearly every bed.

I SAID NO PICTURES PLEASE

Star of *"The World Of Suzie Wong,"* **France Nuyen** slugs it out with photographers at a Miami airport when they insist on taking pictures of her and her travelling companion, **Marlon Brando**.

Crowd and reporter shy **Ava Gardner** irritates the Australian press by refusing to show up for a scheduled press conference.

HOLLYWOOD DESIGNER DON LOPER Voices His Dissatisfaction With **PRINCESS GRACE'S** Look Created By Paris Designers Saying That She Was More Glamourous When He Dressed Her.

THEY DON'T WANNA COME UP AND SEE HER SOMETIME

CBS Cancels Scheduled "Person To Person" Airing Of Charles Collingwood's Interview With **MAE WEST** After CBS Officials Decide The Show Is "Too Hot To Handle."

LIBERACE Is Awarded $22,500 In Damages In His Libel Suit Against The London "Daily Mirror" Over A Column Written By William Neil Connor Implying That He Is A Homosexual.

As Leading Lady GINA LOLLOBRIGIDA Looks On In Horror, Actor Luis Santana Bursts Into Flames On The Set Of King Vidor's "Solomon and Sheba" When He Brushes Against A Flaming Brazier.

Following A Year's Absence From Baseball Following A Crippling Car Accident That Ended His Career, **ROY CAMPANELLA** Takes A Job As East Coast Assistant Supervisor Of Scouting For Los Angeles Dodgers As Well As Spring Training Coach At A Salary Of $25,000 A Year.

DON'T SPEND IT ALL AT ONCE, ELVIS

Elvis Presley is promoted from Private First Class to Specialist Fourth Class with a monthly pay hike from $108.37 to $135.30.

ELVIS IS ALIVE AND WELL AND STILL WEARING HIS BLUE SUEDE SHOES

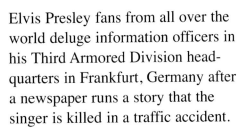

Elvis Presley fans from all over the world deluge information officers in his Third Armored Division head-quarters in Frankfurt, Germany after a newspaper runs a story that the singer is killed in a traffic accident.

A SAD ENDING FOR ONE WHO BROUGHT SO MUCH HAPPINESS

63-year old surviving member of the Abbott & Costello comedy team, **Bud Abbott**, doesn't have much to smile about these days. The IRS wants $500,000 in back taxes and Bud says he's broke. To make matters worse, they have forced him to put his house up for sale and Bud is wondering where have all his pals gone.

Indian Prime Minister Nehru gives refuge to the Dalai Lama, spiritual and temporal ruler of Tibet, along with thousands of his countrymen who were forced to flee their country after Red China stamped out rebellion in the remote mountain land making Tibet the Hungary of Asia.

In further developments, Nehru and India are further beset by Red China's claims to frontier territory leading to armed clashes along the Tibetan border.

The Struggle Continues

In Seclusion In India, Tibet's Exiled Dalai Lama, 24, Decides To Step Out To See A Showing Of "The Ten Commandments" Which He Very Much Enjoys.

Mount Everest Conqueror Sir Edmund Hillary Is Refused Entry In Tibet By The Chinese Communist Government.

In a Cinderella story, 21-year old former maid, *Anne Marie Rasmussen* marries *Steven Rockefeller* in a tiny, unpretentious rural church in Norway.

Reporters and 5,000 well-wishers gather to witness this fairy-tale moment.

Governor and Mrs. Rockefeller (right) and Mr. & Mrs. Rasmussen gather on the steps of the church following the ceremony.

In keeping with Norwegian tradition, the couple did not kiss during the ceremony but they do so for the American cameramen.

The beaming couple wave to the crowd who wish them a happily-ever-after ending.

In a somewhat more pretentious wedding, SHAH PAHLAVI OF IRAN takes a third wife, marrying beautiful commoner 21-year old Farah Diba, with the hope that she will present him with a son and heir to the thousands of years-old throne.

Thrice-Wed Zsa Zsa Gabor Returns 42-Carat Blue-White Diamond Engagement Ring To California Builder Hal Hayes, Stating That She Needed To Be Swept Off Her Feet.

⋯ ⋉⋈⋊ ⋯

Debbie Reynolds Grants Her Husband, Eddie Fisher, The Right To Get A Quickie Nevada Divorce So He Can Marry Elizabeth Taylor, Which He Does 3 1/2 Hours After The Divorce Becomes Final.

⋯ ⋉⋈⋊ ⋯

In Court To Get His Ex-Wife To Comply With His Visitation Rights, Marlon Brando And Anna Kashfi Do Not Look At Each Other But Agree Through Their Attorneys To An Out-Of-Court Settlement.

⋯ ⋉⋈⋊ ⋯

Jimmy "The Schnoz" Durante, 66, Unmarried Since The Death Of His Wife In 1943, Announces His Engagement To Margie Little, 38, With The Wedding To Take Place Next Year.

COUPLING

Claire Bloom & Rod Steiger

Brigitte Bardot & Jacques Charrier

Terry Moore & Stuart Cramer

Margaret O'Brien & Harold Robert Allen, Jr.

Elliott Roosevelt, Jr. & Jo Anne McFadden

Joe Louis & Martha Jefferson

Elizabeth Taylor & Eddie Fisher

Charles Coburn & Winifred Natzka

Stan Freberg & Donna Jean Andreson

George Sanders & Benita Hume Colman

Gene Krupa & Patricia Bowler

Julie Andrews & Tony Walton

Vivian Blaine & Milton R. Rackmil

Ernest Borgnine & Katy Jurado

James Coburn & Beverly Kelly

Dorothy Malone & Jacques Bergerac

Dorothy Dandridge & Jack Denison

Victor Mature & Adrienne Joy Urwick

Sammy Davis, Jr. & Loray White

UN COUPLING

Hugh Hefner & Millie Williams
Arlene Dahl & Fernando Lamas
Esther Williams & Ben Gage
Marlon Brando & Anna Kashfi
Debbie Reynolds & Eddie Fisher
Billy Rose & Joyce Matthews
Otto Preminger & Mary Gardner Preminger
Sammy Davis, Jr. & Loray White Davis
Rod Steiger & Sally Gracie
Mickey Rooney & Elaine Mahnken
John Drew Barrymore & Cara Williams
Ernest Borgnine & Rhoda Kemins
Anita Ekberg & Anthony Steele
Betsy Drake & Cary Grant
June Lockhart & John Lindsay
Glenn Ford & Eleanor Powell
Deborah Kerr & Anthony Bartley
Vera Miles & Gordon Scott
Veronica Lake & Joseph A. McCarthy
Audrey Meadows & Randolph Rouse

MONEY DIDN'T BRING HER HAPPINESS

Aristotle Onassis Sued For Divorce By His Wife Of 13 Years, Tina Mary Onassis.

After A 10-Year Marriage, Diva Maria Callas, 35, And Her Husband, Giovanni Meneghini, 64, Announce Their Separation.

Heiress Gloria Vanderbilt Battles It Out In Court With Ex-Husband Leopold Stokowski Over Custody Of Their Two Children.

WHAT DO YOU THINK HE'S DOING... HAVING A PICNIC?

Separated From His Third Wife, Betsy, Hollywood Hunk Cary Grant Attends The Grand Finale Of The Cannes Film Festival With Beautiful Kim Novak Where They Danced, Danced, Danced, All Night.

On his state visit to the U.S., Soviet Premier Nikita Khrushchev gets to see the filming of "Can Can" and meets Shirley MacLaine, Frank Sinatra, Maurice Chevalier and Louis Jourdan. Citing security reasons, however, and much to his chagrin, the Soviet leader is barred from Disneyland.

★ New England Poet **Robert Frost,** Four-Time Pulitzer Prize Winner, Celebrates His 85th Birthday Predicting That Senator Jack Kennedy Will Be The Next President Of The United States.

★ Poet **Carl Sandburg** Mesmerizes A Joint Session Of Congress As He Expounds On The 150th Birthday Of Abraham Lincoln.

CHURCHILL

Despite Warnings From His Doctor, Winston Churchill Schedules U.S. Trip To Visit With President Eisenhower.

HOW LOW CAN YOU GET?

Thieves make off with Lady Churchill's jewelry and furs and if that isn't bad enough, they also steal three boxes of the former prime minister's favorite cigars.

Winston Churchill Wins Seat In Parliament Making Him One Of The Oldest Members.

Sir Winston Churchill Celebrates His 85th Birthday Surrounded By His Ten Grandchildren, Champagne And A Cake Containing One Candle For Each Year.

Sir Winston Churchill's Daughter, Sarah, Is Arrested In London For Public Drunkeness And Fined $5.60.

THE WHITE HOUSE REVISITED

Celebrating their 40th anniversary, the Women's National Press Club gives a *"Life With Father"* luncheon and tour of the White House with Mamie Eisenhower, inviting the children of former presidents including Major John Eisenhower, John Coolidge, James Roosevelt, Richard Cleveland, Mrs. Alice Roosevelt Longworth, Mrs. Helen Taft Manning, Mrs. Marion Cleveland Amen and Mrs. Eleanor Wilson McAdoo.

IS YOUTH WASTED ON THE OLD?

A Gallop Poll shows presidential hopeful Democratic Senator **John Kennedy** would be defeated by New York Governor Nelson Rockefeller. The young Senator receives other discouraging news slipping behind Adlai Stevenson in New Jersey as voters voice their concern that Kennedy is too young to lead our Allied leaders who range in age from 60's (Harold Macmillan, Charles de Gaulle) to 80's (Konrad Adenauer).

An early Gallop Poll indicates that **Richard Nixon** could easily defeat Senator John Kennedy or Adlai Stevenson.

President Eisenhower gives presidential hopeful Democratic Senator John Kennedy's campaign a boost saying that he didn't know if a Catholic could be elected president but that a candidate should not be barred simply because he is Catholic.

Governor Rockefeller withdraws as a 1960 presidential candidate.

Mrs. Eleanor Roosevelt Guest Of Honor At London Luncheon, Along With Her Granddaugher Nina, Attended By Lady Churchill And Former Prime Minister Clement Attlee To Launch The British Edition Of Her Autobiography.

21-Year Old Granddaughter Of Nationalist Chinese President Chiang Kai-shek Quietly Enrolls At Mills College In Oakland, California.

New York Governor Rockefeller's Norwegian Daughter-in-Law Anne Marie Enrolls In Columbia University For An Intermediate English Course For Foreigners.

OH PLEASE GRANDMA, I'D WALK A MILE FOR THIS ONE

Visiting A Bazaar In Beersheba, Israel With Her Famous Grandmother, **Mrs. Eleanor Roosevelt**, 16-Year Old Nina Falls In Love With A Baby Camel Whom She Names "Duchess" And Implores Her Granny To Buy it For Her, Which She Does For $77.00.

England's peppery Field Marshall Montgomery is warmly

greeted by Soviet Premier Nikita Khrushchev for two days of private talks on a wide range of world affairs.

Montgomery's unofficial visit is viewed with loud apprehension by the British press as earlier he had announced that American leadership of the free world has deteriorated.

Montgomery recants and gives a mild apology for belittling American leadership and said he is optimistic that war over Berlin can be avoided.

IN A RADIO AND TELEVISION SPEECH To The Nation, President Eisenhower Reports That Wherever He Went On His 11-Nation Tour He Found A Deep Longing For Peace.

SON OF THE ARMY'S First Black General Officer, Air Force Brigadier General Benjamin Oliver Davis, Jr. Is Nominated By President Eisenhower For Promotion To Two-Star Rank Which Would Make Him The Highest-Ranking African American In U.S. Armed Forces History.

JIMMY STEWART AWARDED RANK Of Brigadier General By The Senate Armed Services Committee Ending An Air Force Two-Year Battle With Senator Margaret Chase Smith Who Had Been Blocking The Promotion.

U.S. ADMIRAL R. L. Dennison Is Appointed Supreme Allied Commander In The Atlantic.

THE U.S. SENATE CONFIRMS The Appointment Of Ogden R. Reid As U.S. Ambassador To Israel.

POPE JOHN XXIII Appeals To World Leaders To Work For Unity And Peace In His First Encyclical.

No other Jet to Europe offers you the extra comfort of Pan Am's exclusive first-class lounge.

Halfway to Europe between cocktails and coffee

Don't plan to catch up on your reading. There's too much to take in—too much to talk about on your first Jet Clipper* flight.

While the stewardess removes the last cordial glass from your dinner table, she reminds you to set your watch five hours ahead and tells you that there's barely enough time to finish a chapter before you see the lights of London.

Pan Am Jets are fastest to London, the only Jets to Paris and Rome. And this summer, Pan Am is increasing its schedules to include as many as four Jet flights a day to Europe—with deluxe *President Special* service available on every one. You can also fly economy-class Clipper Thrift service, if you wish, with fares starting as low as $453⁶⁰† round trip.

For reservations, call your Travel Agent or any of Pan Am's 61 offices in the U. S. and Canada.

*Trade-Mark. Reg. U.S. Pat. Off. †Fares subject to change.

World's
Most Experienced
Airline

*Pan Am Jet Clippers...world's fastest airliners...the only economy-class Jet service...
the only Jets to all three capitals: London, Paris and Rome.*

ERNEST HEMINGWAY

Celebrates His 60th Birthday In Spain By Going To A Bullfight.

After Nearly 1,500 Performances In New York And London As Eiza Doolittle, "My Fair Lady's" Julie Andrews Sings To Professor Higgins For The Last Time.

Prima Donna Maria Callas receives a dozen curtain calls after her peformance in "Medea" in London's Covent Garden. All performances are sold out with the most expensive seats ordinarily selling for $11.76 being scalped at $70.

Banned from the Metropolitan Opera, Calllas performs brilliantly in concert at Camegie Hall under the auspices of the American Opera Society with ticket prices as high as $33 per ticket.

Painter **Pablo Picasso** donates two paintings for Paris auction to benefit flood victims in the French Riviera town of Frejus and urges other artists to make similar contributions.

81-year old cellist **Pablo Casals** declares "rock 'n' roll a disease that will pass away as quickly as it was created."

Marlene Dietrich

Makes Her Singing Debut At Paris' Etoile Theatre
With Jean Cocteau, Lena Horne, Orson Welles And Maurice Chevalier There To Cheer Her On.

Dietrich, The Most Glamourous Grandmother In The World, Faints As Argentine Fans Mob Her To Show Their Affection.

* 20-Year Old Cigar-Smoking **Shelagh Delaney** Hailed As Britain's Answer To Francoise Sagan On The Opening Of Her Play "A Taste Of Honey," Which Is Quickly Picked Up By American Producer David Merrick For A Broadway Debut.

* Author Of The Nobel Winning Novel "Dr. Zhivago," Russian Poet-Novelist **Boris Pasternak** Attends A Performance Of The New York Philharmonic Conducted By **Leonard Bernstein** And Lavishes Great Praise On Mr. Bernstein.

* Michigan Supreme Court Justice **John D. Voelker** Turns In His Bench For A Typewriter Having Earned $500,000 For "Anatomy Of A Murder," Written Under His Pen Name Robert Travers.

* American Primitive Painter **Grandma Moses** Celebrates Her 99th Birthday.

TAKE A SHOT AND WE'LL CALL YOU IN TWO DAYS

When immigration officials discover his smallpox vaccination has expired, "Auntie Mame" author **Patrick Dennis** is denied re-entry into the United States and detained for 48 hours on returning from a 6-week tour of Russia.

✳ Contralto **Marian Anderson** Becomes First Black Member Of Manhattan's Elite Cosmopolitan Club For Women.

✳ **Kristoffer Kristofferson**, Brilliant 22-Year Old Rhodes Scholar From Pomona College In Southern California, Answers Ad In London's "Daily Mirror" For Young Musicians And Winds Up With A Recording Contract With J. Arthur Rank's Top Rank Records And Is Renamed Kris Carson.

✳ Bandleader Benny Goodman Presents The N.A.A.C.P.'s Spingarn Award For Highest Achievement By A Black American To Jazz Great, **Duke Ellington**.

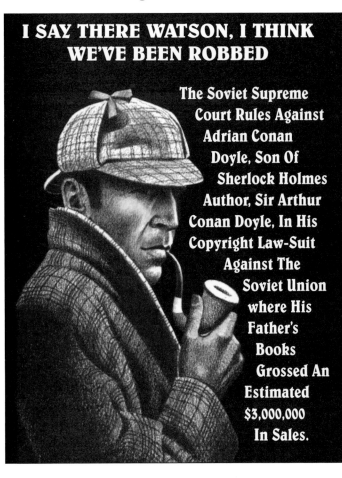

I SAY THERE WATSON, I THINK WE'VE BEEN ROBBED

The Soviet Supreme Court Rules Against Adrian Conan Doyle, Son Of Sherlock Holmes Author, Sir Arthur Conan Doyle, In His Copyright Law-Suit Against The Soviet Union where His Father's Books Grossed An Estimated $3,000,000 In Sales.

Good Dog!

Rather Than Put Them In An English Kennel, *Noel Coward* Sends His Two Poodles To A Swiss Boarding School Where They Will Be Instructed In Good Manners And How To Behave Like Gentlemen.

Robert Anderson, **Herbert Hoover**, **Marian Anderson**, **James R. Killian** And **Frank Pace, Jr.**, Receive National Institute Of Social Sciences Gold Medals.

President Eisenhower Awards The Medal Of Freedom To **John Foster Dulles**, The Highest U.S. Civilian Award.

The National Institute Of Social Science Presents Its 1959 Gold Medals For Distinguished Service To Humanity To **Dr. Jonas Salk** (Polio Vaccine,) **Helen Hayes** (Actress) And **Laurance Rockefeller** (Financier.)

Violin Virtuoso **Jascha Heifetz**, 58, Becomes Full Professor Of Music At The University Of California At Los Angeles.

Nobel Prize winner 84-year old **Albert Schweitzer** goes to Copenhagen to receive a Sonning Prize, the Danish equivalent of the Nobel Prize, which brings with it a cash award of $14,250 which the missionary-physician will use for his famous jungle hospital in Gabon, Africa.

The Sole Survivor Of The Family That Lived In Mortal Fear Of Being Discovered In Hidden Quarters Of A House In Amsterdam, Concentration Camp Survivor **Otto Frank** And His Second Wife, Elfriede, Tour New York After Attending A Special Showing Of **"The Diary Of Anne Frank,"** A Film Based On The Diary Of His Young Daughter. Mr. Frank Plans To Establish A Youth Center In Anne's Memory In The Same Building Where The Family Hid From The Nazis.

HOW MUCH DO YOU THINK WE'LL GET FOR PARK PLACE?

A New York judge rules that four of the children of Boston millionaire **Joseph P. Kennedy** are entitled to a fair price for one of their buildings which was condemned to make room for New York City's new Lincoln Center and so **Mrs. Jean K. Smith**, **Mrs. Peter Lawford**, **Mrs. Eunice Shriver** and **Robert Kennedy** get to divvy up $2.4 million, which is the amount the judge awarded them for the property.

HENRY AND ANNE FORD Spend An Estimated $100,000 On Their Daughter Charlotte's Coming Out Party Attended By Anyone Who's Anyone From The United States And Europe.

Spiritual Head Of 20 Million Ismaeli Moslems, 22-Year Old Karim Aga Khan IV Receives His BA From Harvard University And The University Receives $50,000 From Aga Khan For Scholarships To Middle Eastern Students.

Evangelist Billy Graham spends five months preaching in Australia and New Zealand despite problems with one of his eyes.

First Female President Of The Federal Aeronautique Internationale, U.S. Aviatrix Jacqueline Cochran, Presides Over First Meeting Of This Organization Ever Held In The Soviet Union.

SOMETHING TO MAKE A BIG RACKET ABOUT

Ralph **Bunche**, Nobel Peace Prize Winner and present United Nations Undersecretary for Special Political Affairs, intercedes unsuccessfully on behalf of his 15-year old son, Ralph, when he is refused membership in New York's West Side Tennis Club in Forest Hills. The club's president, Wilfred Burglund, said Forest Hills does not allow African Americanss or Jews to join this prestigious club.

Public outrage is vociferous, U.S. senators issue a public statement condemning the racist practices of the West Side Tennis Club and faced with an investigation by the New York Commission on Interfaith Relations, the club's president resigns and a new policy is passed that accepts membership without regard to race, creed or color.

BEAUTY CONTEST WINNERS

MISS AMERICA
Mary Ann Mobley, 21, Brandon, Mississippi.

Tokoyo's **Akiko Kojima** becomes first Asian to win the **MISS UNIVERSE** title while New York model, 20-year old **Cecilia Cooper,** becomes first black woman to become France's annual Cannes Film Festival's **MISS FESTIVAL**

MRS. AMERICA
Mrs. Margaret Priebe, Des Moines, Iowa.

18-year old secretarial student **Pat Williams** becomes first black woman to become **MISS SACRAMENTO**

Indiana University sophomore **Nancy Street** has a lot to smile about as she is the first black woman to become a beauty queen on that campus.

Sigma Chi member **Warren Beatty** graduates Northwestern University.

Timothy Leary joins the faculty of Harvard University.

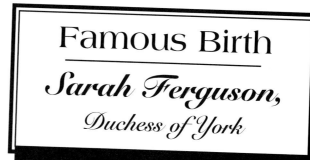

Famous Birth
Sarah Ferguson, Duchess of York

PASSINGS

Lead defense attorney in the famous Scopes "monkey" trial, **John R. Neal**, age 83, dies in Tennessee.

Joseph Barbara, in whose Apalachin, New York home the infamous meeting of dozens of underworld members took place, dies at 53 of a heart attack.

1959 ADVERTISEMENT

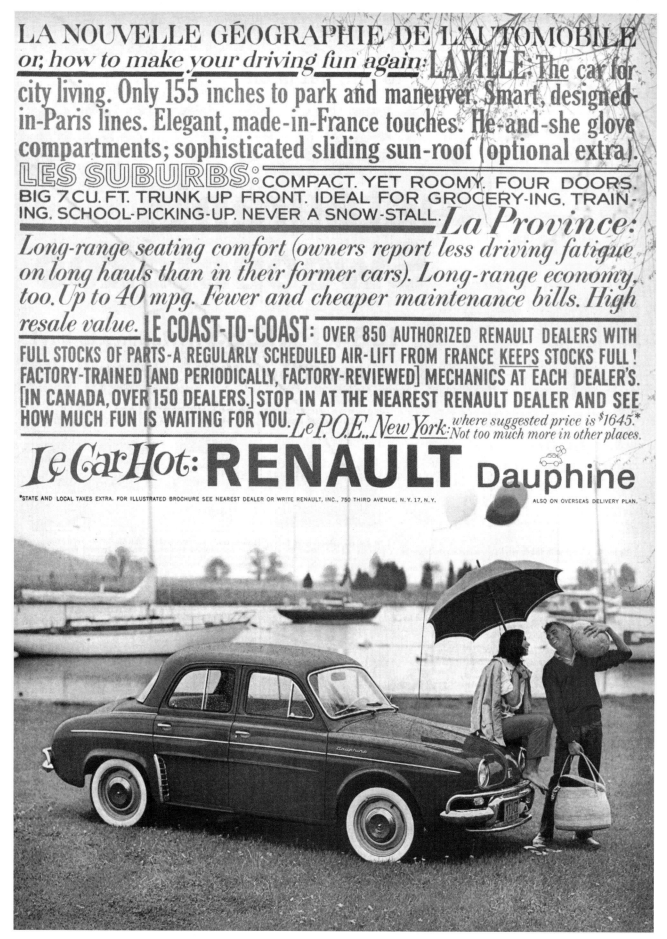

LA NOUVELLE GÉOGRAPHIE DE L'AUTOMOBILE *or, how to make your driving fun again:* LA VILLE: The car for city living. Only 155 inches to park and maneuver. Smart, designed-in-Paris lines. Elegant, made-in-France touches. He-and-she glove compartments; sophisticated sliding sun-roof (optional extra). LES SUBURBS: COMPACT. YET ROOMY. FOUR DOORS. BIG 7 CU. FT. TRUNK UP FRONT. IDEAL FOR GROCERY-ING. TRAIN-ING. SCHOOL-PICKING-UP. NEVER A SNOW-STALL. *La Province:* *Long-range seating comfort (owners report less driving fatigue on long hauls than in their former cars). Long-range economy, too. Up to 40 mpg. Fewer and cheaper maintenance bills. High resale value.* LE COAST-TO-COAST: OVER 850 AUTHORIZED RENAULT DEALERS WITH FULL STOCKS OF PARTS-A REGULARLY SCHEDULED AIR-LIFT FROM FRANCE KEEPS STOCKS FULL! FACTORY-TRAINED [AND PERIODICALLY, FACTORY-REVIEWED] MECHANICS AT EACH DEALER'S. [IN CANADA, OVER 150 DEALERS.] STOP IN AT THE NEAREST RENAULT DEALER AND SEE HOW MUCH FUN IS WAITING FOR YOU. *Le P.O.E., New York:* *where suggested price is $1645.* Not too much more in other places.*

Le Car Hot: **RENAULT** Dauphine

*STATE AND LOCAL TAXES EXTRA. FOR ILLUSTRATED BROCHURE SEE NEAREST DEALER OR WRITE RENAULT, INC., 750 THIRD AVENUE, N.Y. 17, N.Y.   ALSO ON OVERSEAS DELIVERY PLAN.

HUMAN INTEREST

Usually blase Londoners can't help but stare with amusement at this **space-age smog mask**.

The inventor says it is very practical and that all social amenities can be observed such as **kissing**

and **eating and drinking**.

Reader's Digest remains No. 1

in circulation followed by **LIFE**, **LOOK** and the *Saturday Evening Post*.

New York Herald Tribune columnist,

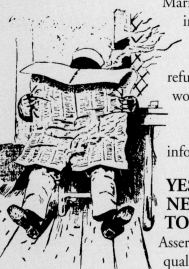

Marie Torre, is thrown in jail for 10 days for contempt of court after she refuses to testify which would have compelled her to reveal confidential information.

YESTERDAY'S NEWSPAPER TODAY

Asserting that the quality of running and printing on wastepaper is the same as "new paper," the **Chicago Sun-Times** announces the use of 10,000 tons of wastepaper in its daily editions.

"Lady Chatterly's Lover"

is banned from the U.S. mails on grounds the book is obscene.

Upholding first amendment rights

in the case involving "**Lady Chatterly's Lover**," New York court rules that New York cannot constitution-ally prevent the exhibition of a motion picture because the content might be contrary to popular moral, religious or legal standards.

The Clutter Family Of Holcomb, Kansas Are Found Brutally Murdered In Their Home.

- A Special Task Force Created By New York's Police Commissioner To Fight Upsurge In Youthful Offenders.

- - - - - - - -

- The Latest FBI Reports Reveals That Los Angeles Has More Crime Than Chicago Or New York.

- - - - - - - -

- Fort Lauderdale, Florida Beefs Up Its Police Force And Sets Up A Police Station Right On The Beach In Anticipation Of College Spring Break.

HEY LET'S TEACH KIDS NON-VIOLENCE BY PADDLING THEM IN OUR SCHOOLS

Much To The Frustration Of The Mothers Who Demand A Warrant, Memphis Sessions Judge Willard Dixon Refuses To Issue Warrant For The Arrest Of John Barnes, Principal Of Bartlett High Who Paddled 14 Children.

MEANWHILE, BACK IN CIVILIZATION...

New York Governor Nelson Rockefeller Vetoes "Hickory Stick" Bill Pushed Through The State Assembly Authorizing Paddling Of Students As A Means Of Punishment.

the doublemint twins make their television debut.

- Dan Enright, One-Time Producer Of Six Television Quiz Shows, Including "Tic Tac Dough," "Dotto" And "Name That Tune," Testifies Before Congress That In Order To Increase Ratings, Quiz Shows Have Been Rigged For Years Down To Rehearsed Emotions And Advance Answers To Questions.

- FCC Issues Equal Time Ruling Requiring TV To Give A Forum To All Political Candidates.

- A Los Angeles Judge Grants A Divorce To A Hollywood Actress On The Grounds That Her Husband Watches Too Much Television.

New Flowers That Bloom In The Spring

PRAIRIE DAWN: Pink double blossoms, no fragrance, very hardy and will thrive on prairies.

STARFIRE: Large double medium, moderate fragrance, red flowers that bloom in candelabra-like clusters.

GOLDEN GIRL: Golden yellow double flowers, moderate fragrance, light green foliage.

GARDEN PARTY: Pale yellow double blooms with slight fragrance.

400 American schools will offer Russian in their curriculum.

Massachusetts Superior Court Judge Jennie Loitman Barren is named Mother Of the Year by the American Mothers Committee.

Philosopher Hannah Arendt writes essay advocating same-sex marriage.

THEY'LL BE DANCIN', DANCIN' IN THE STREETS

10,000 Out Of The Estimated 1,000,000 Square Dancers In The U.S. Converge On Denver For The Eighth Annual National Convention Of Square Dancers.

New Dance Crazes - **The Dog, The Shag And The Alligator** Are Banned As Being Too Provocative.

HOT DANCES

Cha-Cha   Mambo

American Teenagers Are Less Interested In Rock 'n' Roll Dancing But Their Japanese Counterparts Are Real Enthusiasts.

The Newest of Everything Great! ——— *The Greatest of Everything New!*

Design you out? No, Never!

Comfort stages a comeback. You get it in oversize doors, unobstructed entrance space, deeper seat cushioning, greater headroom. As an extra note of grace, add Dodge's new Swing-Out swivel seats.*

Now, it's nice to ride low and snug-to-the-road. You are more secure. The car is in better command.

But here's something important to you. When Dodge pioneered the low Swept-Wing car, you were designed *into* it, not *out* of it.

We figured that *solid comfort* for driver and passengers is something you're entitled to *along with lowness and beauty and style.*

The way you *get* in it, the way you *sit* in it, sets this '59 Dodge apart from the field.

We're talking about *more* than the new Swing-Out swivel seats*. We mean the size of the door opening and the clearance for your head and shoulders and knees and feet when you enter.

We mean the support under your legs, the deep cushioning at your back, the position of your body when you settle down.

This '59 Dodge was built around *you.* That is one mark of a great car. Compare it!

optional at extra cost

'59 DODGE

Dodge brings you Lawrence Welk on television every week, ABC-TV network. Ask your Dodge dealer for time and channel.

Chicago's 61st Annual Automobile Show

Showcases A Glittering Array Of Vehicular Innovations

Everything you'll see on the highway in the months ahead is shown including this swivel seat *(left)* and a handy headrest for those long sunday drives *(right)*.

There's a new Japanese addition to the ranks of the little foreign cars which are becoming increasingly more popular in the U.S.

This particular model has a folding bed inside.

The First Urban Monorail System In The United States Commences Operation In Tomorrowland.

Matterhorn Mountain Opens For Bobsled Business.

The 15th Millionth Person Enters Disneyland.

Costing A Whopping $2.5 To Build, The SUBMARINE VOYAGE Is Opened.

The E Ticket Is Born

Disneyland News

WHAT'S NEW IN NEW YORK?

President Eisenhower gives New York approval for 1964 World's fair in Flushing Meadow, choosing New York over Washington and Los Angeles.

The city comes to an electrical standstill as Manhattan loses its power during a sweltering heat wave.

New York's Ebinger bakery chain goes on strike and New Yorkers muddle through yet another crisis - being deprived of their pumpernickel or their Jewish rye bread. Oy.

New York's Grant's Tomb becomes a national shrine.

Ground is broken in New York for the $320 million Verrazano Narrows Bridge.

Construction begins on the lower deck of the George Washington Bridge.

New York has the largest population in the country followed by Chicago and Los Angeles.

- Plans Are In The Works For A Three-Stage Rapid-Transit System Including A Subway Under The Bay Between San Francisco And Oakland.

- Pittsburgh Celebrates Its Bicentennial With A Major Effort In Rebuilding The City.

- Farmers Market In Los Angeles Is #2 Tourist Attraction With Disneyland Holding The #1 Spot.

The Tancarville, longest suspension bridge in Europe, spanning the Seine River near Le Havre France, opens for its first crossings.

In preparation for man's first space voyage,

seven astronauts of Project Mercury, space men of tomorrow, experience the eerie sensation of total weightlessness in special training flights.

First Round-The-World Jet Passenger Service Is Kicked-Off By Pan-American Airways.

Construction Begins On The New Jet Airport At Chantilly, Virginia To Be Named Dulles International Airport.

FAA Rules Commercial Pilots Must Turn In Their Wings At Age 60.

The U.S. Air Force Academy In Colorado Springs, Colorado Graduates Its First Class.

France's Only Woman Test Pilot, Jacqueline Auriol Breaks Her Own World Air Speed Record Flying At 1,344 m.p.h. At 37,000 Feet, Almost Double Her Former Speed.

BY THE SKIN OF HER MAST

With less than seven foot clearance, the INDEPENDENCE, world's largest aircraft carrier, barely makes it under the Brooklyn Bridge as she sets out for her first sea trial.

UNSAFE AT LOWER SPEEDS

The Lowest Accident Rate Occurs At 65 MPH With Three Times As Many Accidents At 35 M.P.H.

Contrary To Popular Opinion, Women Are Not The Worst Drivers But Military Personnel Are With Five Times As Many Accidents As Civilians.

Laws Preventing School Integration Are Struck Down By Virginia Supreme Court And Segregated Schools In Arlington And Norfolk See Their First Black Students.

Georgia Is Directed by federal courts to end segregation of its public schools.

Florida admits several black students to Miami's Dade County all-white schools.

Arlington And Norfolk Virginia desegregate public schools without violence.

FOLLY of FAUBUS

Governor Orval E. Faubus closes high schools in Little Rock, Arkansas in protest over federal court desegregation rulings.

U.S. Supreme Court overturns Arkansas law that allowed Governor Orval Faubus to close public high schools.

The riot squad is called out as a violent mob tries to prevent integration of Central High in Little Rock, Arkansas.

Local police enforce order as five black children enroll in Little Rock public schools after Governor Faubus accedes to federal court ruling.

ATLANTA BUSES AND TROLLEYS are desegregated without violence.

WITH REGISTERED VOTERS BEING WHITE ONLY in a county that is 50% black, a Mississippi circuit appeals court ruling to overturn the murder conviction of a Black is upheld by the Supreme Court.

FEDERAL REGISTRARS TO OVERSEE VOTING in the south requested by Civil Rights Commission.

U.S. SUPREME COURT overturns Louisiana's ban on boxing matches between whites and blacks.

FOUR YOUNG WHITE MEN are tried and convicted of raping a black girl and are sentenced to life imprisonment.

AT A CONVENTION IN NEW YORK celebrating the NAACP's 50th anniversary executive secretary Roy Wilkins cites the achievements of the organization including the end of lynchings and the breaking down of color barriers.

Mother Elizabeth Seton (1774-1821)

Mother Elizabeth Anne Seton

first American to be beatified by the Catholic church.

GET THEE TO A CHURCH

B-3 I-4 N-27 G-7 O-6. BINGO IS LEGALIZED IN NEW YORK.

EVANGELICAL LUTHERANS and United Evangelical Lutherans join forces forming the American Lutheran Church.

ACCORDING TO THE UNITED COUNCIL OF CHURCHES, 64% of Americans belong to a church.

GIVE ME THAT OLD TIME ROCK 'N' ROLL

The congregation of Rev. Geoffrey Beaumont drinks beer and dances to rock 'n' roll hymns in his St. George's Anglican Church in London.

NO REDS IN THE ROSARY
The Pope decrees Catholics may not support the Communist party.

IT ISN'T RAINING RAIN YOU KNOW, IT'S RAINING ROCKS

A hailstorm strikes Oklahoma dropping stones more than 10 inches in diameter.

THE CITY DOESN'T WANT TO GET TRIPPED UP Mobile, Alabama passes an ordinance requiring women to obtain a high-heel license which absolves the city from damages.

COME ON FELLAS, SUCK IN THOSE TUMMIES

TELEPHONE

In keeping with the national fad, 22 students of St. Mary's College in Moraga, California sardine themselves into a telephone booth but fail to break the record of 25 established in the Union of South Africa.

Over a 4 month period a series of eruptions occur at Kilauea Iki Crater on the island of Hawaii. Lava is catapulted more than 1,000 feet into the air in one of the most spectacular eruptions of the 20th century.

CRAMMING CALIFORNIA STYLE

Having run out of loose change, students at California's Long Beach State College decide to switch from cramming into phone booths to trying their luck at cars and some 40 of them pile in (and out of) a Volkswagen.

NEW WORDS &

AMBUCOPTER
A helicopter utilized as an ambulance.

DECOUPLING
A way to conceal a nuclear blast.

ELECTRONIC FENCE
When planes and other carriers make an imaginary fence.

BEER-B-QUE
A barbecue that has beer as its prime refreshment.

DENUCLEARIZATION ZONE
An area where nuclear tests will be prohibited.

FALL-IN
Radioactive waste from peaceful purposes.

BUDGET BUSTER
An individual who spends more money than they have.

DE-SMOGGING
To eliminate smog-generating particles from automobile exhaust.

GO-KARTING
Go-kart racing.

HALF-JAIL
Where an alcoholic lives in the evening, but is allowed to leave for work.

COLD SLEEP
Hypothermia.

DISCOMFORT INDEX
A way of measuring a person's discomfort due to weather conditions.

HOT ISSUE
Stocks that will increase in price when publicly sold.

COMPUTERESE
Codes observed by a computer to decipher problems.

DUBBIDOBBER
A section of the X-15 rocket's ejection seat.

HULA HOOP DISEASE
Neck and abdominal pain found in hula hoop users.

COSMIC ROCKET
A rocket that forever leaves the earth's gravitational pull.

EVANGELIZE
To proselytize.

JETWALK
A walkway that takes passengers from the terminal to the airplane.

EXPRESSIONS

JUNGLE MARKET
When the rules of the jungle dominate business.

OUT-PRICE
To offer lower prices.

PLANETEER
One who voyages in space.

MECHTA
The name of the first Russian rocket to reach solar orbit.

PADDLE WHEEL SATELLITE
Nickname for the Explorer 6.

REVERSE PROGRAMMING
To reschedule a program at a different time than similar programming.

MICRO-SLEEP
Short relaxation periods during the day.

SALES KIT
The procedure of entertaining a potential client.

MOON HOUSE
A home for human moon dwellers.

PAGODA
A new architectural home style.

SLALOM
A type of water ski.

SOCIAL HANG-OVER
The self-conscious feeling one has the day after a wild party.

NYMPHETITIS
Fear of advanced sexual displays.

PAPERIZE
To add to office procedures.

THINK CONTRACT
A contract focusing on theoretical labor.

OPEN CURTAIN
Business transactions with Russians.

VALET PARKING
When an attendant parks and retrieves a patron's automobile.

WONNY
A veteran of World War I.

111

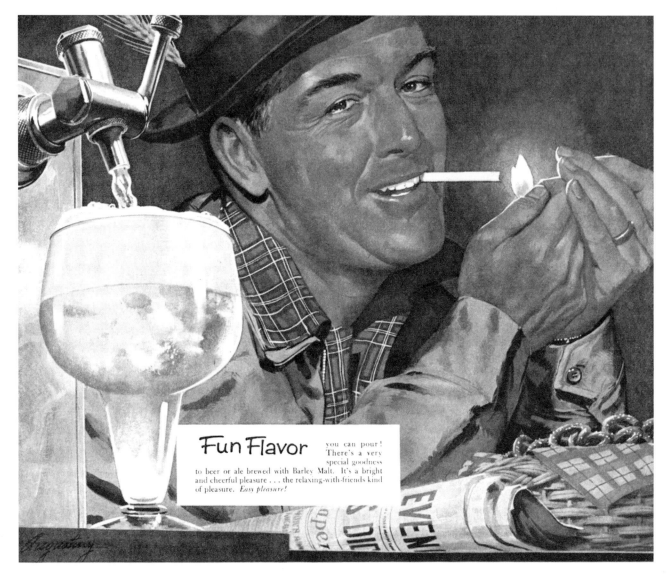

Fun Flavor you can pour! There's a very special goodness to beer or ale brewed with Barley Malt. It's a bright and cheerful pleasure ... the relaxing-with-friends kind of pleasure. *Easy pleasure!*

The goodness of Malt
adds a premium to pleasure

Barley *and* Malt
INSTITUTE

whose members are U.S. malting companies that guide sun-ripened barley through a natural process with scientific care to insure the goodness of Malt.

MALT'S HEALTHFUL VALUES are the welcome premium you enjoy in scores of Fun-Flavored foods and beverages. The maltose and dextrins of Barley Malt aid digestion ... pick up lagging energies.

GOOD-FOR-YOU FACTORS include important B-complex vitamins and useful minerals. Good reason to look for Barley Malt in cereals, dairy drinks, baked goods, energy tonics and many other healthful products.

Write for free booklet, Homemaker's Guide to Barley Malt, Dept. 3, Barley & Malt Institute, 228 North LaSalle, Chicago 1, Illinois.

WE HAVE OUR MEMORY PRIORITIES IN ORDER

Most Americans polled know who utters *"Hi Yo, Silver"* and *"What's Up Doc?"* but did not know who said *"I Have Not Yet Begun To Fight"* (John Paul Jones).

Martha Brunner Of Pittsburgh, Pennsylvania Is "Little Miss Muffin For 1959" In A Contest Sponsored By The Associated Retail Bakers Of America.

HEAD OF THE CLASS(ES)

According to Dr. Harold M. Hodges, Jr., a sociologist at San Jose College, American society now consists of five social classes instead of three: **upper, upper-middle**, **lower-middle**, **upper-lower** and **lower-lower**.

U.S. POPULATION: 179 MILLION

Marriages: 1,494,000

Divorces: 396,000

HEY BUDDY, WE'VE GOT THIS GREAT DEAL ON SWAMP LAND

Land fever sweeps through Florida with lots of lots being sold via the mails.

Former President Harry S. Truman's Birthplace In Independence, Missouri, Is Dedicated As A National Shrine.

According to a recent study, most Americans want love and appreciation over wealth and fame.

According to the New York Stock Exchange, 13 million Americans own stock.

The Statue Of Liberty Celebrates Her 75th Birthday.

☭ U.S. And Soviets Will Exchange Artists In The Performing Arts For Exhibitions To Be Held In New York And Moscow.

☭ The United States And The Soviets Agree On Cultural Exchange Including Arts, Science And Sports.

☭ Pravda, The Soviet Newspaper, Treats Its Readers To The First Cartoon Of A Soviet Leader To Appear In The Russian Press.

'TILL MOSCOW FREEZES OVER

The First American Ice Show Goes To Russia.

HUSBAND HUNTING MADE DIFFICULT

A New Census Report Taken In The U.S.S.R. Reveals That There Are 55 Females For Every 45 Males.

A PEROGY ON EVERY PLATE?

CIA Director Allen Dulles Challenges Khrushchev's Prediction That The U.S.S.R. Would Boast The World's Highest Standard Of Living In 11 Years.

DIVORCE EAST GERMAN STYLE

In East Germany a divorce can be granted on the grounds of "Anti-Marxism."

With More Than 10,000 East Berliners Streaming Into West Berlin Monthly, East Germany Becomes The Only Country In The World With A Steady Decrease In Its Population.

Volkswagen Factories Returned To Private Ownership In West Germany.

A Salvage Team Discovers Nazi Gestapo Chief Heinrich Himmler's Personal Files And Diaries In Austria's Toplitz Lake.

DON'T LOCK HORNS WITH THIS COUNCILWOMAN
Protesting against the high cost of living, the electorate in Rio de Janeiro vote for their favorite write-in candidate for city council - Cacareco, the rhinoceros, who gets more votes than any other candidate. The winner is single and presently lives in the zoo.

NEXT THEY'LL BE WANTING SHOES

A constitutional amendment granting women voting privileges in national elections is defeated 2-1 by Swiss men.

3,500 WOMEN RECEIVE THE RIGHT TO VOTE in the sixteeenth century old town of San Marino near Italy's Adriatic coast.

6,500 SYLVANIA FLASH BULBS erupt into one blinding burst as the 451-foot high Great Pyramid in the desert outside of Cairo is totally illuminated and photographed.

AMERICANS FAVOR CANADA
as their vacation destination over any other country in the world.

WHAT'S AN EIGHT LETTER WORD FOR BUSTED?

A ring of Americans and Canadians guilty of cheating on newspaper word puzzles by getting the answers in advance is broken up by the FBI.

Queen Elizabeth and President Eisenhower preside over the opening of the St. Lawrence Seaway, the world's greatest inland navigation system linking the Great Lakes to the Atlantic. Canada's icebreaker "d'Iberville" unofficially opens the Seaway.

Tols are established for the St. Lawrence Seaway.

n An All-Out Effort To Get Brits To The Polls On Election Day, British Commercial Television Cancels All Western Programs That Day.

BEN JUST KEEPS TICKING AWAY
London's Big Ben Celebrates Its 100th Anniversary

The First Telephone Cable Linking North America And Europe Becomes Operational

NOT MUCH FIDDLIN' AROUND THESE DAYS

Nero's Garden Ruins Discovered In Rome By Archaeologists.

SO WHAT'S BEEN HAPPENIN' MAN?

The First Greek Ruler Since 1439 Calls On The Pope.

- **Heir to Jordan's Kingdom, Amir Mohammed,** opens Aqaba, a Jordanian port.

- **Italian workers begin digging a tunnel** through Europe's highest mountain, Mont Blanc, which will decrease driving distance from Paris to Milan by several hundred miles.

- **Mexico and the United States** agree to build Diablo Dam on the Rio Grande.

- **Over 55 million women and children** in 105 countries receive help from UNICEF.

- **The International Red Cross turns 100.**

- **The Hague, Netherlands** is the home of the newly-formed International Society For Horticultural Science.

- **Spanish Jews** celebrate their first Rosh Hashana services in Madrid for the first time in 467 years.

- **World Refugee Year** commencing June 1959 is proclaimed by the U. N. General Assembly.

A 12-Nation Pact Is Signed In Washington Declaring Antarctica A Military-Free Preserve For Scientific Research.

After two years of animal testing which produced evidence of injury, the Food And Drug Administration bans 17 coal-tar dyes used to color lipsticks.

BARKING UP THE RIGHT TREE

In an effort to quiet down the loud barking at the Toronto Humane Society, keepers of the pound begin playing Benny Goodman and Liberace recordings. The result: the dogs wagged their tails, tapped their paws and ceased their barking ways.

An elephant believed to date back to the ice-age is discovered while digging on a farm in Lafayette, Indiana.

PUT AWAY THOSE FISHING POLES, BOYS

In an action designed to protect its wildlife, the government of Ecuador declares the Galapagos Islands a national park with limited fishing rights in and around the waters surrounding the islands which are designated a marine sanctuary.

The London Zoo presents 12 flamingos to Queen Elizabeth.

Scientists warn the Blue Whale could be extinct in five years unless restrictions are placed on the international whaling industry.

According to a recent report released by a Chicago bank, married women are better money managers than their husbands and make most of the buying decisions.

SOME SAY "I DO" AND THEY DO, WHILE SOME SAY "I DO" AND THEY DON'T

18% of American first marriages end in divorce—that's one in six—and one-third of second marriages also end up on the rocks.

SHOULDN'T WE WAIT UNTIL OUR ZITS GO AWAY?

Teenage marriage (14-19-year olds) on the rise since World War II.

American Girls Marry At Youngest Age Of Industrialized Nations, 20.2, While The Men Marry By Age 23.

RAISING THE ODDS

Chances For A Successful Marriage Are Higher When Men Marry Between Ages 25 To 30 And Women Between 23 To 28.

Polls indicate that most parents do not want their teenagers going steady too soon because of the emotional pressures it places on them.

RULES OF GOING STEADY

1. Exclusivity *(no dating others)*
2. Dancing only with each other *(unless they exchange dances with another couple)*
3. He can't leave her without a Saturday night date
4. He telephones her every night *(or has a reason why not)*
5. She must be at home to receive his call *(or has a reason why not)*

TRAITS THAT WILL KEEP YOU HOME EVERY SATURDAY NIGHT:

Exaggerate or lie

Use foul language

Insist on having last word

Unreliable

Pout when you can't have your own way

Drink too much

Make disparaging remarks about older people

Exhibitionist behavior

Make negative comments about men

YOU ARE VERY DATABLE IF....

Weight and height in proportion.

Graceful bearing, stable and confident.

Neatly groomed hair and nails.

Sensible makeup.

Flattering clothing.

Tasteful accessories.

Pleasing voice.

Good sense of humor.

Good dancer.

Good listener.

HI HONEY...WHOOPS I MEAN HELLO SIR!

ATT&T develops the call director, a new 18-button phone capable of receiving multiple calls through an illuminated push-button panel, allowing calls to be placed on hold while another call is answered. It's also an intercom system for up to 29 office extensions.

Two Belgian inventors develop Teledial, a gadget that recalls and automatically dials phone numbers.

RCA develops a small radio phone the size of a shoe box and weighing less than 10 pounds.

THE GIFT OF SPEECH

Bell Telephone invents a transistorized artificial larynx allowing people with damaged vocal cords to speak.

Bell Telephone Laboratories is assigned patent of inventor Floyd F. Becker of Summit, New Jersey for his television telephone invention.

DIALING IN THE DARK

A new telephone which has the dial in an illuminated handpiece, is being tested in the New Jersey area by the Bell Telephone Co.

WALK, WALKED... DONE WALKED

Karl A. Pansch Develops A Machine That Helps Students Conjugate Irregular English Verbs.

29-Year Old MIT Researcher, Douglas T. Ross, Develops Mechanical Brain With 107-Word Vocabulary For Use In Automation.

Called The Beginning Of The Second Industrial Revolution, RCA And The Army Signal Corps Develop A Micromodule Which Will Greatly Reduce Electronic Products As 27 Of These Chips Can Be Placed In Only One Cubic Inch Of Space.

Tidewater Oil Comes Up With A New Gasoline Which They Claim Causes Less Pollution.

An Electronic Addition To Vending Machines Gives Change After Purchases.

Electronic Banking Begins In California.

A remote-controlled typewriter designed for paralyzed people who operate the machine through their head and neck muscles is developed.

The Federal Communications Commission grants permission for private citizens to have two-way radios creating the Citizen Radio Service providing 22 radio channels.

As lightweight as a regular watch is what the Bulova Watch Co. is saying about their new electronic wristwatch.

SUGAR & MILK FOR BREAKFAST

Frosty O's, General Mills' New Breakfast Cereal, Is Showing Up In Breakfast Bowls Across The Country.

New Streamlined One-Piece Packaging Is Developed For Frozen Foods Replacing The Bulky Double Package.

ATTENTION SHOPPERS: SPECIAL TODAY...

"Store Video," A Closed-Circuit In-House Advertising Tool For Supermarkets Will Soon Be In Your Favorite A & P.

Westinghouse Designs The Dog-O-Matic—

An Appliance That Can Cook Six Frankfurters In Just 90 Seconds.

Metrecal Diet Drink *Introduced By The Mead Johnson Co. Is A Hit.*

JUST FOLLOW THAT YELLOW LINE

Minnesota Mining & Manufacturing develops an illuminating paint for airport runways and taxi strips.

SAN FRANCISCO INTERNATIONAL AIRPORT

initiates use of first "Jetwalk" in the nation developed to protect passengers from weather conditions by allowing them to board airplanes through a telescoping indoor corridor.

Even Motorcycle Cops Hiding In The Bushes?

General Motors Develops Experimental Car Equipped With Radar Equipment To Warn Drivers Of Road Hazards.

A New Speed-Control Device For

Highway Driving Is Developed By The Glide Control Corporation Of Inglewood, California.

If I Could Only Find The Knob On This Fa-Schunkt-Kaner Machine

Facing Loss Of Their Licenses For At Least Five Years For Drunken Driving, Germans Take Advantage Of A New Machine At Their Neighborhood Tavern Which For Only 50 Pfennigs ($ .12 U.S.) Measures The Blood Alcohol Level.

Chevrolet Corvair

Becomes First American Car With Engine In The Rear.

130

Science

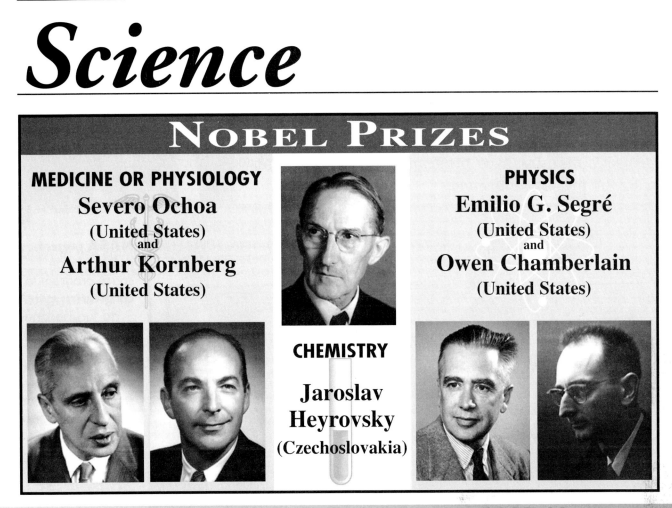

NOBEL PRIZES

MEDICINE OR PHYSIOLOGY
Severo Ochoa
(United States)
and
Arthur Kornberg
(United States)

CHEMISTRY
Jaroslav Heyrovsky
(Czechoslovakia)

PHYSICS
Emilio G. Segré
(United States)
and
Owen Chamberlain
(United States)

A Social Scientist From The University Of Michigan predicts that **SCIENTIFIC ADVANCES** will **PEAK IN 1973** and then **SLOW DOWN** around the year **2055**.

MY SON, THE PROFESSOR

UNIVERSITY OF CALIFORNIA PROFESSOR, HANS ALBERT EINSTEIN, son of Albert, is honored by the American Society of Civil Engineers for outstanding research on transportation of sediment in flowing water.

A LOOK AT THE WORLD AT THE TURN OF THE CENTURY
—— Y E A R   2 0 0 0 ——

Scientists at the Stanford Reseach Institute report on the rapid development of peacetime science and suggest the following are among the many sobering results of present research:

1. Rocket Mail Service
2. Synthetic Coffee & Tea
3. Climate Control
4. Radio Broadcasts Relayed By Space Satellite
5. Teaching Machines
6. Brain Control
7. Mine The Ocean Floor
8. Further Development Of Oral Contraceptives
9. Chemical Food Pills

WHAT THEY NEED IS W.A. [WATER ANONYMOUS]

Britain reports on the "Hydrolic," a compulsive water drinker who consumes 30 - 35 pints of the clear stuff a day and exhibits many of the same outward symptoms of a drunk including the next-day hangover.

CITING EINSTEIN AND FREUD AS EXAMPLES, according to University of Wisconsin genetecist Dr. William Harold Stone, Jews possess superior intelligence precisely because they "have been isolated by geographical, cultural and religious barriers" thus keeping their gene pool from co-mingling with other gene pools which may have less of a propensity for pursuing intellectual or analytical careers.

Successful Testing Is Reported By Nobel Prize Winner, **Dr. John F. Enders** On Children Who Develop Antibodies After Being Given A Live-Virus Measles Vaccine.

❑ French geneticist Jerome Lejeune traces an extra chromosome as the cause of mental and physical handicaps of people afflicted with Down's Syndrome.

❑ HIV tainted blood given by a Bantu man from Central Africa at a hospital clinic in the Belgian Congo.

❑ Frozen bone marrow cells are now available for the first time through a technique developed by the Veterans Administration.

❑ 300 plant and animal viruses have been identified — 80 in the past ten years.

A New Survey Concludes That Salt Is A Major Contributer To High Blood Pressure.

Studying 60 babies with brain damage and their normal counterparts, Dr. Samuel Karelitz, director of pediatrics at Long Island Jewish Hospital, concludes that the cry of a brain-damaged baby is different from the non-brain damaged children in that they don't cry as quickly when stimulated to do so and their cry is spasmodic and irregular.

WHO WEARS THE PANTS IN YOUR FAMILY?

Studies conducted at McGill University indicate children who grow up in homes where the fathers are dominant tend to be more emotionally well-adjusted than those where mothers are the bosses.

Today's Health **magazine** reports that despite medical advances, old wives tales regarding pregnancy still exist such as **if you wear high heels your baby will be cross-eyed** or **if you go out in the rain, the baby will drown** or **if youhave heart-burn your baby will be hairy.**

Babies born to drug-addicted mothers can be addicts themselves and have a lower chance for survival unless diagnosed and treated immediately.

MUSIC DOTH SOOTHE THE SAVAGE CHILD

8-Year Old Disturbed Youngsters Calmed Down Considerably When Soft, Classical Music Is Played In The Classroom According To Tests Conducted By Professor Charles H. Patterson, Jr, Of Longwood College, Farmville, Virginia.

New Jersey's 90-Year Old Statute Limiting The Sale Of Contraceptives Is Held Unconstitutional.

Ground Breaking Research Being Conducted At Stanford Medical Center Gives New Hope To Women Unable To Bear Children Through A New Process Of Fertilization In Which Fertilized Donor Eggs Are Implanted Surgically.

OH BABY!

BETTER NOT BE MORE THAN KISSIN' CUZINS

Researchers Conclude That When First Cousins Marry, The Death Rate For Their Children Is About Three Times Higher Than Unrelated Parents And The Incidence Of Abnormalities Is About Double The Average.

The National Safety Council Reports That 30 Small Children Died In Several Months From Suffocation Caused By Playing With Plastic Bags Precipitating A Nationwide Campaign To Alert Parents To The Dangers Of Allowing Their Children To Play With Plastic Bags Used In Dry Cleaning.

The Traditional RABBIT TEST May Be Replaced With A Newly-Developed Hormone-Pill Test For Pregnancy Promising Much Greater Accuracy.

RESEARCH INTO GIVING ELECTROCARDIOGRAMS to unborn fetuses to detect defects is being conducted at Yale University.

ACCORDING TO AN ARTICLE appearing in Postgraduate Medicine, despite all the modern conveniences at home, the demands of motherhood are greater than ever causing many moms to experience fatigue dubbed tired mother syndrome.

STUDIES AT THE PHILADELPHIA LYING-IN HOSPITAL reveal that taller women give birth to bigger babies.

TRANQUILIZER PHENERGAN used during childbirth to lessen pain.

ONE OUT OF EVERY 5,000 BRITONS are test tube babies.

ACCORDING TO A PEDIATRICIAN at Northwestern University, colicky infants generally emerge as leaders in their adult life.

THE AMA APPROVES HYPNOSIS AS A MEDICAL AID IF ADMINISTERED BY TRAINED PHYSICIANS OR DENTISTS.

DR. A. H. C. SINCLAIR-GIEBEN OF THE UNIVERSITY OF ABERDEEN, SCOTLAND REPORTS EXCELLENT SUCCESS IN TREATING PATIENTS WITH WARTS THROUGH THE USE OF HYPNOSIS CITING 10 OUT OF 14 CASES WHERE THE WARTS DISAPPEARED FROM THE "TREATED" HANDS.

The Army Quartermasters Corp. is testing a line of disposable hospital paper products including nightgowns, sheets and gowns for doctors and nurses.

Hospital staph infections cause great alarm in the medical world as infections sweep through hospitals from nurseries to wards causing deaths.

GOLF WIDOWS SHOULD REJOICE

Men who play golf have lower risk of heart attacks and are generally easier to live with.

$250,000 is allocated by the U.S. Public Health Service for the study of the smog problem in Los Angeles.

SOME LIKE IT HOT OR EVEN HOTTER

Scientific research being conducted at Rutgers University on mosquitoes seems to indicate that they target their meals based on their potential meals' body heat and it seems that skinny people are more appetizing than the fatter ones.

LOVE & MARRIAGE DON'T GO TOGETHER LIKE THE HORSE & CARRIAGE

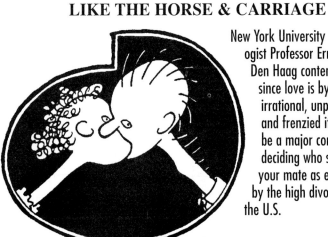

New York University anthropologist Professor Ernest Van Den Haag contends that since love is by its nature irrational, unpredictable and frenzied it should not be a major component in deciding who should be your mate as evidenced by the high divorce rate in the U.S.

According to a joint study conducted by Drs. James B. Hamilton and Gordon E. Mestler, State University of New York and Harumi Terada, Tokyo University, Caucasian women tend to have more facial hair than their Japanese counterparts and older white women tend to grow mustaches, especially if they're French.

Severely depressed women at California's Camarillo State Hospital being given beauty treatments to try to rebuild their self-esteem.

Even though the hormone dramatically relieves symptoms, doctors are hesitant to give menopausal women estrogen because of their concern that it could possibly cause cancer although no definitive research backs up their fear.

Two out of three doctors are women in the Soviet Union.

PSYCHIATRY

Scientific Evidence Seems To Indicate That Mental Powers Don't Decline After Middle Age.

ACTING CAN BE DANGEROUS TO YOUR MENTAL HEALTH

According to a famous Hollywood psychiatrist more than half of Hollywood's actors and actresses will experience mental health problems.

SMILE THOUGH YOUR HEART IS BREAKING

In a study of American entertainers conducted by two sociologists at the University of Texas, it is revealed that while more than one third of America's most successful entertainers experienced difficult childhoods, comedians had the most difficult time as kids, with more than 40% of them coming from broken homes and 70% of them experiencing poverty as youngsters.

Because Of Long Hours Of Isolation, The Personality Type Best Suited For A Spaceman Is An Introvert.

VE VANT TO BE ALONE

A staff psychiatrist for San Francisco's Veterans Hospital defines "Beatniks" as not necessarily sick of life but like any group of sick people just want to be left alone.

The Mental Research Institute of Palo Alto, California begins operation.

According to Dr. Lewis J. Sherman, Veterans Hospital, Brockton, Massachusetts, psychopathic criminals tend to have better memories than normal or neurotic people because the psychopath isn't beset by memory-blocking anxieties.

Philadelphia psychologist Dr. Carlton W. Orchinik notes that children who stutter are more likely to have been tickled hard by a parent of the opposite sex.

According to a report issued by the National Institute of Mental Health, one out of sixteen Americans will suffer a mental illness.

With The Pursuit Of Materialism Coupled With Expanding Technology, Americans And Europeans Are Destined To Suffer From A "Mass Neurosis" Unless The Pace Of Modern Life Slows Down According To A British And A Canadian Scientist.

Ever So Smart, So Debonair*

What is so fair...so brimming with trim, good looks and vitality... as today's up-to-date Americans? They favor the new light look. And everything in the land reflects their preferences.

Move toward the light look. Look smart. Stay young and fair and debonair. Be sociable. Have a Pepsi—the lighter Pepsi of today, reduced in calories.

PEPSI-COLA   the Light refreshment

It's A Living

As the **National Debt** approaches the legal limit fixed by Congress of $295 billion, approximately each of the 176,665,000 Americans will owe roughly $1,641.52 to the future.

FORD DROPS ITS SUPER LEMON THE EDSEL

Labor Department Announces A Record Employment Of 68 Million, Less Than One In 20 Workers Out Of Work. Last Year's Unemployment Rate was 1 Out Of 15.

McCall's Magazine

Becomes First National Women's Magazine To Include A Special Western Edition.

Hormel + Co. Produces Its Billionth Can Of SPAM

U.S. ATLANTIC AND GULF COAST PORTS almost entirely shut down due to International Longshoremen strike.

 IN THE LONGEST NATIONWIDE STEEL STRIKE in America's history, and the 6th since World War II, 500,000 steelworkers strike as their union and management fail to reach an agreement, closing down 85% of the nation's steel output.

 GENERAL MOTORS ceases automobile production due to strike.

 1,100 HOSPITAL EMPLOYEES representing seven major New York hospitals go out on an unparalleled 45-day strike.

 STRIKING AMERICAN AIRLINES PILOTS settle a three-week strike which idles 18,000 other employees resulting in $34 million in lost earnings and salaries.

NEW YORKERS HAVE TO MUDDLE THROUGH for 19 days without their favorite newspaper as a deliverymen's strike closes down the city's nine major dailies with a total circulation of 5.7 million.

 6,000 CHICAGO TEACHERS go on strike for, and win, a $500 annual increase, making them the highest paid city teachers in the country.

*Senator
Robert A. Taft,
author of
Taft-Hartly act.*

Taft-Hartly Injunction to end steel strike ordered by U.S. District Court in Pittsburgh and stayed by U.S. 3rd Circuit Court Of Appeals.

President Eisenhower names a board to inquire into the steel dispute after invoking the Taft-Hartly Act.

Taft-Hartly Injunction against steel strike upheld by U.S. Supreme Court.

Readmission Of International Longshoremen on a two-year probation is authorized by the A.F.L.-C.I.O.

American Federation Of Television And Radio Artists and the Screen Actors Guild vote to merge into one union with a combined membership of 25,000.

Congress Passes First Major Labor Law since the 1947 Taft-Hartly act as a result of the McClellan Committee hearings which investigated union corruption. With Robert F. Kennedy acting as chief counsel, Teamsters' head Jimmy Hoffa is called to testify many times but is evasive and falls under a barrage of criticism for not cleaning up his union.

President Of United Mine Workers since 1919, **John L. Lewis** announces his plan to resign in 1960.

John L. Lewis

Studebaker-Packard joins the small car market with the debut of its Lark model.

- Ford beats Chrysler by a beak as they both register the name "Falcon."

- The success of the Rambler pulls American Motors out of the red for the first time in six years.

- Grand Jury investigation of General Motors under the antitrust laws is ordered by U.S. Justice Department.

American Airlines announces that its Boeing 707 airliners have been flying nearly 100% full.

The Long Island Railroad celebrates its 125th birthday and spruces up its Insignia.

First class and deluxe passengers will now be able to order from 36 different meals being offered on Swissair.

Chemical Corn Exchange And **New York Trust** Merge To Form **Chemical Bank New York Trust Co.** Making It New York's Third Largest Bank.

Two Banking Institutions Merge, **J. P. Morgan Co.** And **Guaranty Trust Co.**, Forming **Morgan Guaranty Trust**, Creating The Fourth Largest Bank In The Country.

BUY NOW AND PAY LATER

The **Bank of America** Introduces The First American Revolving Credit Card Allowing Minimum Monthly Payments With The Balance Carried Over To The Following Month With Interest Added.

Passings

NEWSWEEK creator and heir to one of the great fortunes of all time, businessman and philanthropist **Vincent Astor** dies at age 67.

Chairman of Pepsi-Cola and Joan Crawford's husband, **Alfred N. Steele**, dies of a heart attack in New York at age 57.

The first woman president of Lord & Taylor, **Dorothy Shaver**, dies of a stroke at age 61.

New Jersey Mail-Order House, Free Film Co., Acts As Broker For Several Photo Finishers Providing Free Film

With Developed Pictures To The Consumer Who Skips Their Neighborhood Drugstore, Allowing Them To Save At Least 40% In Developing Charges.

THE DOW-JONES industrial average

passes the 600 mark and continues to rise to 678.10.

THE FUNCTION OF CLEARING TRANSACTIONS for the American Stock Exchange is assigned to a new machine.

FAMILY-OWNED NEIMAN-MARCUS stock is offered to the public for the first time at $19.50.

Growing Demand For

Coconut Oil

Causes Sharp Increase In Price.

A record $68 billion is spent on life insurance.

Los Angeles plans to revitalize its downtown area with the $339 million Bunker Hill project.

A group of American textile machinery companies signs a contract with the Soviet Union to provide and install equipment for spinning and weaving factories.

McDonnell Aircraft in St. Louis is awarded a $15 million space exploration contract.

Ground is broken in Lake Maracaibo, Venezuela for new $3 million flour mill in a joint venture between Pillsbury Co. and Latin American industrialist Eugenio Mendoza Goiticoa.

78% of the nation's 370,000 college seniors have already found jobs with electrical engineers being the most desired for technical positions.

Hollywood Actress **Joan Crawford Steel** *Is Elected To Pepsi-Cola's Board Of Directors To Fill Opening Left By The Death Of Her Husband Alfred, Chairman Of The Board.*

Mrs. Josephine Bay, Financier And Sportswoman Of New York And Palm Beach, Is Elected Chairman Of American Export Lines, Inc. Becoming First Woman To Head Major Ship Line.

PLAYING KETCH-UP

The First Non-Family Member To Become President Of H. J. Heinz Co. Is **Frank R. Armour, Jr.**, *50, Who Started Out As A Visitors' Guide In 1927.*

this is the price that was

UNDER $1.00

Aspirin, 100 ct.	$ .49
Ball Pen	1.00
Carnegie Hall (lowest priced ticket)	.60
Cough Syrup	.49
Eyelash Curler	1.00
Life Savers	.05

Life Magazine	$ .25
Lipstick	.79
Magic Marker	.77
Movie Ticket (child)	.50
Nail Polish	.49
Public Drunkenness Fine (London)	.70
Toothpaste	.88
Tweezers	.29

HOME NECESSITIES

Baby Stroller	$ 24.95
Clothes Hamper	5.95
Fountain Pen	2.95
Mattress, Posturepedic	79.50
Movie Projector	89.95
Play Pen (portable)	24.95
Sewing Machine (portable)	69.50
Stereo	39.95
Radio, transistor pocket	34.95
Television w/remote control	199.95
Vacuum Cleaner	49.50

THE ULTIMATE KITCHEN

Blender	$ 34.95
Double Boiler	11.75
Electric Range	149.00

Iron	$ 16.95
Percolator	17.95
Skillet	16.95
Tea Kettle	4.95
Toaster	29.95

FOR HIM

Boxer Shorts	$ 1.65
Haircut: Los Angeles	2.00
New York	1.50
Shoes	7.95-19.95
Slacks	10.98
Socks	1.00
Sports Shirt	2.99
Suit, worsted	65.00
Tie, silk	2.95
Topcoat	65.00

New York Rentals

5 room apartment in Flushing: $150.00

4 room apartment in Jamaica: $115.00

3½ room apartment in Rego Park: $135.00

2 family house in Bensonhurst: $125.00

FOR HER

Bermuda Shorts	$ 10.95
Capri Pants	5.98
Cardigan	5.98
Dress (Italian wool knit)	35.00
Dress (pleated jersey)	14.98
Espadrilles	2.50
Girdle	12.50
Gloves	4.98
Handbag *(straw)*	$ 16.95
Hat *(velvet & rayon)*	16.95
Housecoat *(silk brocade)*	25.00
Pedal Pushers	4.98
Petticoat	5.99
Shoes *(imported)*	30.95-45.00
Toreador Pajamas	6.95

AUTOMOBILES

Edsel Station Wagon	$ 2,971.00
VW Bug	1,675.00
Mercedes Benz, 300 SL Roadster	10,978.00
Volvo	2,390.00
Jaguar Mark IX	6,200.00

FOOD

American Cheese *(lb.)*	$ .51
Apples *(lb.)*	.16
Butter *(lb.)*	.77
Coffee *(lb.)*	.78
Corn *(10 ears)*	.25
Honeydew Melon *(ea.)*	.59
Iceberg Lettuce	.19
Milk *(qt.)*	.27
Oreo Cookies *(11 oz.)*	.33
Peanut Butter *(12 oz.)*	.35
Sugar *(lb.)*	.11
Vegetable Oil *(qt.)*	.45
Watermelon *(lb.)*	.04

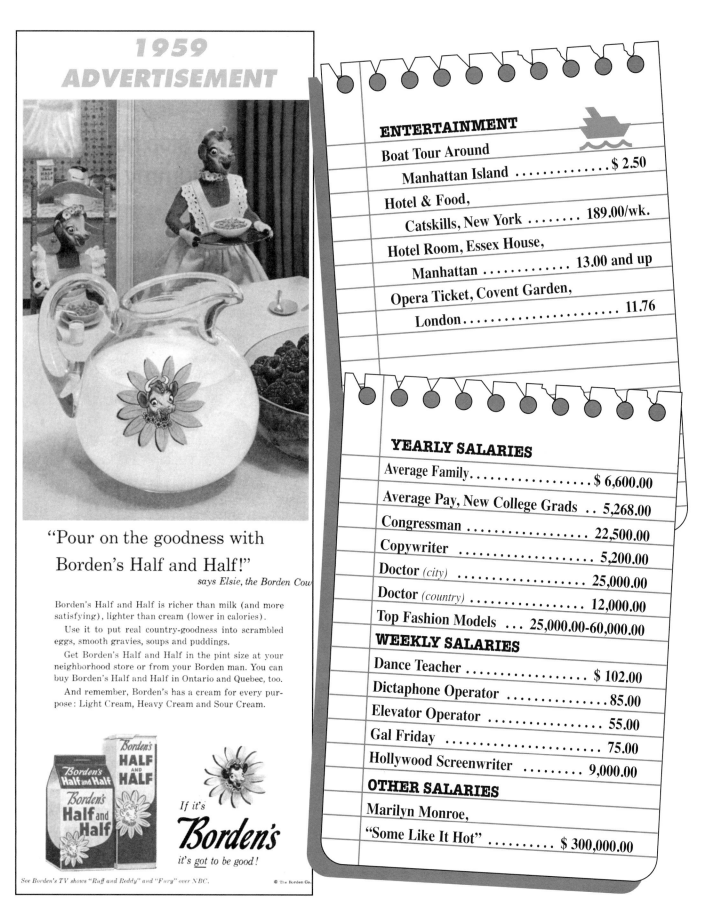
ENTERTAINMENT

Boat Tour Around
    Manhattan Island . . . . $ 2.50

Hotel & Food,
    Catskills, New York . . . . 189.00/wk.

Hotel Room, Essex House,
    Manhattan . . . . 13.00 and up

Opera Ticket, Covent Garden,
    London 11.76

YEARLY SALARIES

Average Family. . . . . $ 6,600.00
Average Pay, New College Grads . . 5,268.00
Congressman 22,500.00
Copywriter 5,200.00
Doctor *(city)* 25,000.00
Doctor *(country)* 12,000.00
Top Fashion Models . . . 25,000.00-60,000.00

WEEKLY SALARIES

Dance Teacher . . . . $ 102.00
Dictaphone Operator 85.00
Elevator Operator 55.00
Gal Friday 75.00
Hollywood Screenwriter 9,000.00

OTHER SALARIES

Marilyn Monroe,
"Some Like It Hot" . . . . $ 300,000.00

Fashion

Italy unveils its fashion fo

FASHION

This clever
3-piece
combination
includes top, pants
and matching
jacket.

La bella signorina starts the day ready for anything in this chic daytime dress that with a twist of the wrist lets her get into the swim of things.

This Japanese
influenced outfit
decorated with
butterflies seems
appropriate since
Madame Butterfly
came from Italy.

swim, sun, fun

And for you gals who want to do a little hip trimming, this ruffled suit could do the trick.

Italian fashions have proven quite popular across the oceans.

IT'S A WELL DRESSED FASHION WORLD

PARIS
The French fashion world is all agog over designer Jules Francois Crahay's first comprehensive collection for Nina Ricci, especially his plunging necklines and sensual curves.

MOSCOW
At the United States Exhibition, Muscovites get a glimpse of how average American adolescents dress. Jeans, sweaters and leather jackets make up some of the casual outfits.

NEGEV
Israeli fabrics continue to gain popularity in clothing designs.

LONDON
Hats with built in air-conditioning are available to avoid breathing unhealthy air.

NEW YORK
The Soviets send over some of their top designers with new creations.

in FASHIONS ENGLAND

DESIGNER NORMAN HARKNELL INTRODUCES HIS NEW LINE FOR FALL AND WINTER.

Traditional British strong points, woolens and tweeds, are very much in evidence in this beautiful suit.

This tweed suit with matching plaid coat, along with the entire collection, will be featured at the gala Scottish industry's exposition later this year.

Two more outfits in wool complete the show demonstrating British artistry at its finest.

Appropriately this stunning ball gown in pure silk satin (above) is richly embroidered with a motif of Scottish roses in gold and crystal.

Continuing the highland's theme, another evening dress in shirting material brightened with the MacBeth Tartan.

Arlene Francis, escorted by Joseph Cotton, Maggie McNellis (left) A (center) and Claudette Colbert and Charles Boyer (right) are among some of the stars participating in this very special event.

March Of Dimes Gala

Some 1,200 people crowd the grand ballroom at New York's Waldorf Astoria for the nation's most famous fashion show – the 15th annual edition of the March Of Dimes style event.

On stage, one-half million dollars worth of the latest spring fashions are paraded by celebrities turned models.

The real stars of the evening are the March Of Dimes poster children who are brought on stage by Jimmy Durante – a reminder that the purpose of this glamorous evening is the support of the foundation's fundraising for research against this crippling disease.

Gliding down the runway with grace and charm are the first lady of American Theatre, Helen Hayes (right) and the vivacious Celeste Holm (left).

157

A short jacket over matching dress with long handbag, gloves and hat.

Silk dress with pleated skirt, a polka dot belt and scarf, sheer hose and low pumps.

The shirtwaist dress, a perennial favorite, acquires a dash of glamour and can now be worn in the evening.

WINTER, SPRING, SUMMER or FALL
– Look Good Through Them All.

Winter: Short sleeve coat with over-sized buttons.

Spring: Light blue chiffon blouse under hip-length jackets.

Summer: Cotton shirt and capri pants with an over-sized straw hat.

Fall: Wool jersey dress with a short jacket in wool or silk.

GIRLS ARE GIDDY OVER GINGHAM...

And wear dresses and bathing suits made of the checkered material.

NIFTY KNICKKNACKS

Clothes may make a personal statement, but it's the jewelry that finishes the outfit. For an evening out, a multi-stranded crystal necklace and a large rhinestone pin in the shape of a flower mix well with a mesh handbag. Daytime is a fine time for a simple pearl necklace with matching bracelet and earrings.

Henry Fonda's pretty daughter **Jane** is a model for **Vogue** magazine.

SHOES

Comfort in women's shoes is an important part of this year's footwear. Pointed toes and high heels give way to lower heels and rounded toes. Ankle boots with flat heels are worn with dresses and suits. A novel idea is the heel-free shoe, made for those who are light on their toes.

PUT YOUR BEST FACE FORWARD

A '59 face is made up with false eyelashes, white shadow and foundation with the sparkling substance guanine.

A new cream with placenta extract is guaranteed to moisturize and revitalize your skin.

Ultra-Feminine, by Helena Rubenstein, is a moisturizer that has estrogen and progesterone as key ingredients.

The Makeur is the mechanical way to put on make-up and creams with ease and accuracy.

The natural look is fine and dandy – as long as it's created with flattering make-up.

HAIR

Hair styles include the bouffant, soft waves, bangs, French twist and dips. Women begin growing their hair long, wearing it down or stacking it atop the head with jewelry. Those feeling nostalgic for yesteryear can try wearing their hair as Greta Garbo did decades ago.

IT'S WIGGY, MAN

Low-priced wigs in wild shades such as purple and red sell thousands a day.

MEN'S FASHIONS

The blucher and wing tip are two ways to top the toes.

The bowler hat is back on top.

The single-breasted Continental suit gains in popularity, giving the Ivy look competition. Wash and Wear suits become more affordable than ever before.

Indian madras is an excellent choice for a lightweight sports coat.

A SURREY WITH THE FRINGE ON TOP...

Sears, Roebuck & Company joins the toupee business, and offers its male customers a varied selection of quality rugs in the $200 range.

Britain's "Tailor and Cutter" magazine chooses an eclectic and international group of men for their yearly best-dressed list. Fred Astaire, Marshall Tito, Richard Nixon and Rex Harrison are among those whose tailored togs keep them looking snappy. At the other end of the spectrum another British magazine, "Man About Town," lists musicians Liberace and Elvis Presley as amongst the world's worst-dressed fellas.

Sports

Baseball

FOR THE FIRST TIME IN MAJOR LEAGUE HISTORY, TWO ALL-STAR GAMES ARE PLAYED For The Benefit Of The Players' Pension Fund With The National League Beating The American League 5-4 In The First Game And The American League Getting Even In The Second Winning 5-3.

Most Valuable Player

National League:

Ernie Banks (Chicago)

American League:

Nellie Fox (Chicago)

ROOKIE OF THE YEAR
NATIONAL LEAGUE
WILLIE MCCOVEY (SAN FRANCISCO)
AMERICAN LEAGUE
BOB ALLISON (WASHINGTON)

CY YOUNG AWARD WINNER
EARLY WYNN (WHITE SOX)

SEASON HOME RUN KINGS
NATIONAL LEAGUE
ED MATHEWS (MILWAUKEE 46 HOME RUNS)
AMERICAN LEAGUE
ROCKY COLAVITO (CLEVELAND 42 HOME RUNS)
HARMON KILLEBREW (WASHINGTON 42 HOME RUNS)

BATTING CHAMPIONS
NATIONAL LEAGUE
HANK AARON (MILWAUKEE .355 AVERAGE)
AMERICAN LEAGUE
HARVEY KUENN (DETROIT .353 AVERAGE)

⚾ Candlestick Park Is Officially Selected As The Name Of The New Giants Ballpark In San Francisco.

⚾ Dodgers Pitcher **Sandy Koufax** Ties Bob Feller's Single Game Strike Out Record And Sets New Two-Game Record.

⚾ **Branch Rickey** Named President Of The Newly Formed Continental League, Baseball's Third Major League.

⚾ Los Angeles Dedicates New Sports Arena Adjacent To Memorial Coliseum.

⚾ Pittsburgh Pitcher **Harvey Haddix** Throws A 12-Inning Perfect Game Against The Milwaukee Braves.

The Martians Are Coming, The Martians Are Coming

Boston White Sox owner, Bill Veeck, stages a mock martian helicopter landing and "abduction" of Nellie Fox and Luis Aparicio at Chicago's Comiskey Park.

⚾

Some Days You Just Shouldn't Get Out Of Bed

Cincinnati pitcher Willard Schmidt is forced to leave a game against the Milwaukee Braves after being hit by two pitches, one batted ball and finally a line drive.

PASSINGS

Owner of the unmatched pitching record of 464 innings in one season, baseball Hall of Fame member **Ed Walsh** dies at age 78.

Napoleon Larry Lajoie, baseball Hall of Famer and greatest second baseman in history, dies at 83.

SPORTS

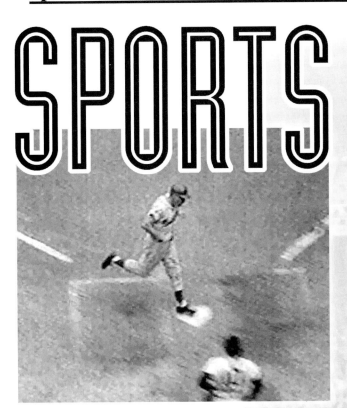

The AL League Pennant Comes To Chicago And The White Sox Are In The World Series For The First Time In 40 Years. Too Bad They Lose To The **Los Angeles Dodgers 4-2.**

Game 2 At Comiskey Park, Dodger Charlie Neal Hits A Home Run And As White Sox Outfielder Al Smith Goes For The Ball An Enthusiastic Fan Accidentally Spills His Beer All Over Smith.

In The Sixth Game Los Angeles Explodes With Duke Snider's Third Inning Homer For A 2-0 Lead.

Celebrating The Dodgers' Win Are Larry Sherry (left) And Duke Snider.

On The Mound To Finish It Off For The Dodgers Is Larry Sherry Who Is Involved In All Four Los Angeles Victories.

From Seventh Place Last Season, The Dodgers Rebounded To The Top And Win The World Series Beating The White Sox 4-2, The First Team In Major League History To Make Such A Dramatic Comeback.

BASKETBALL

The East (Dark) Takes On The West (White) In The 9th NBA All-Star Game Played In Detroit.

Minneapolis Rookie Elgin Baylor Shows A Play That Entitles Him To Share In The Outstanding Player Award For This Game.

1.

3.

The Favored East Fights Back As Boston's Bob Cousy Gets The Ball And Despite A Leg Injury Is In Great Form.

2.

Cousy's Shot Hits The Rim But Bill Russell, Another Celtic, Taps It In.

Later In The Game, Cousy Steals The Ball From Slater Martin Of St. Louis And Scores Again.

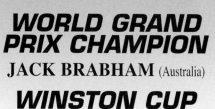

4.

The West Pulls Off A Late Rally With Pettit's Long Pass To Jack Twyman For An Easy Lay-Up And Wins 124-108.

5.

AUTO RACING

WORLD GRAND PRIX CHAMPION

JACK BRABHAM (Australia)

WINSTON CUP CHAMPION

LEE PETTY

INDIANAPOLIS 500 WINNER

ROGER WARD

driving a Leader Card Special 500 Roadster at average speed of 135.857 mph collects $106,850 cash prize.

BASKETBALL

NATIONAL BASKETBALL ASSOCIATION CHAMPIONS
Captain Bob Cousy Leads Boston Celtics
To Championship Beating
Minneapolis Lakers 4-0.

NBA MOST VALUABLE PLAYER
Bob Pettit
(St. Louis)

N.C.A.A. TITLE
Golden Bears Edge West Virginia
71-70 Giving The Pacific Coast
Conference Its First Win Since 1942.

NBA ROOKIE OF THE YEAR
Elgin Baylor
(Minneapolis)

NBA SCORING CHAMPION
Bob Pettit
(St. Louis)

Wilt Chamberlain wins Golden State rookie award.

Elgin Baylor refuses to play in Charleston when a hotel turns away black teammates.

NBA adopts protective policy that demands hosting city not practice segregation of any of its players.

CHESS

WORLD CHESS CHAMPIONSHIP
Mikhail Botvinnik, USSR

America's 16-Year Old Champion
Bobby Fischer Finishes Fifth In
The Final Standing In The World
Challenger's Chess Tournament
Held In Yugoslavia.

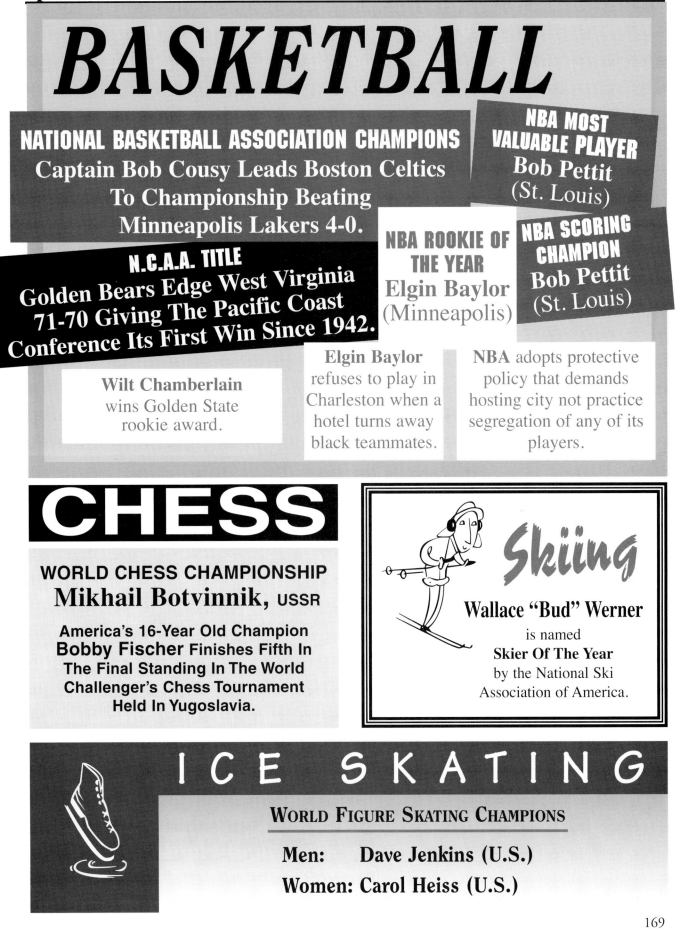

Skiing
Wallace "Bud" Werner
is named
Skier Of The Year
by the National Ski
Association of America.

ICE SKATING

WORLD FIGURE SKATING CHAMPIONS

Men: **Dave Jenkins (U.S.)**
Women: **Carol Heiss (U.S.)**

FOOTBALL

BALTIMORE COLTS Beat **NEW YORK GIANTS 31-16** Winning **National Football League Championship**

PROFESSIONAL PLAYER OF THE YEAR

(OUTSTANDING 1959 NFL PLAYER)

JOHNNY UNITAS
QB, Baltimore Colts

National College Football Champion

SYRACUSE

Heisman Trophy Winner

BILLY CANNON
(HB)
LSU

Army and **Air Force** kick off their rivalry in New York's Yankee Stadium going head to head in a 13-13 tie with 67,000 fans rooting for their favorite.

Over 98,000 fans watch as **Iowa** beats **California** 38-12 winning the **Rose Bowl** championship.

NCAA RULE CHANGES

Increase the space between the goal posts by 4′ 10″ to a total width of 23′ 4″.

Increase the number of allowable time-outs from four to five in each half.

NATIONAL FOOTBALL LEAGUE'S MANAGER OF THE YEAR
Vince Lombardi

Lamar Hunt forms the American Football League.

William "Billy" Sullivan buys Boston Patriots, an AFL franchise, for $25,000.

The Buffalo Bills become the American Football League's seventh team when franchise is awarded to Ralph C. Wilson.

PASSINGS
One of the people responsible for making football a major spectator sport due to his profitable television policies, Bert Bell, former commissioner of the NFL, dies at 65.

SOCCER

The **McIllane Canvasbacks** of San Pedro, California win the United States Challenge Cup beating the **Fall River Massachusetts** team **4-3.**

10,000 fans turn out in Indianapolis to watch heavyweight champion **Floyd Patterson** slash away at his fourth challenger Britain's **Brian London**.

In the 9th round a thunderous barrage of body blows brings down London's guard and cracks open the defense of the 10-1 underdog.

Late in the 10th round, London goes down on one knee after a smashing right high on the cheek but the bell rings on the count of 5 saving the challenger.

Trainers revive London after the round 10 knock down.

London is under blistering fire and a smashing hook drives him across the ring for the K.O. in the 11th round.

BOXING
WORLD TITLES

HEAVYWEIGHT
INGEMAR JOHANSSON
Johansson knocks down current champ, Floyd Patterson, seven times in the third round winning the heavyweight title.

MIDDLEWEIGHT
GENE FULLMER

WELTERWEIGHT
DON JORDAN

LIGHT-HEAVYWEIGHT
ARCHIE MOORE

LIGHTWEIGHT
JOE BROWN

PASSINGS

Former Heavyweight champ, **Max Baer**, dies at 50.

Tony Canzoneri, holder of world championships in three weight divisions (Jr. Welterweight, Featherweight and Lightweight), dies at 51.

CASSIUS CLAY fights his first amateur bouts.

Bowling

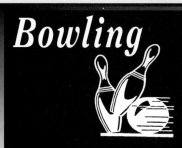

AMERICAN BOWLING CONGRESS CHAMPION

All Events: **Ed Lubanski** Detroit, Michigan
2,116 points.

WOMEN'S INTERNATIONAL BOWLING CONGRESS CHAMPION

All Events: **Pat McBride** Grand Rapids, Michigan
Scores 1,927 points, breaking a 25-year old record.

HORSERACING

WILLIE SHOEMAKER Rides TOMY LEE To Kentucky Derby Win.

HORSE OF THE YEAR: Sword Dancer (with Eddie Arcaro usually riding, Sword Dancer is #1 earner at $537,004.)

HARNESS HORSE OF THE YEAR: Bye Bye Bird

Turf history is made at Churchill Downs with the sensational finish of the Kentucky Derby.

Tomy Lee and Sword Dancer engage in one of the greatest home stretch duels ever producing the only foul claim in Derby history. Tomy Lee wins the run for the roses.

Track & Field Sensation Of The Year

is the 7´ 1-1/4˝ high jump of John Curtis Thomas at Madison Square Garden.

The 17-year old Boston University freshman beams as he sets a dazzling new world record.

James E. Sullivan
Memorial Trophy
Awarded For
Outstanding Sportsmanship
Parry O'Brien (Track)

ICE HOCKEY

CALDER MEMORIAL
(Rookie Of The Year)
RALPH BACKSTROM
Montreal

ART ROSS TROPHY
(Leading Scorer)
DICKIE MOORE
Montreal

LADY BYNG MEMORIAL TROPHY
(Most Gentlemanly Player)
ALEX DELVECCHIO
Detroit

HART MEMORIAL TROPHY
(Most Valuable Player)
ANDY BATHGATE
New York

STANLEY CUP
Montreal Canadiens Beat Toronto Maple Leafs 4-1 For Win.

VEZINA TROPHY
(Outstanding Goalie)
JACQUES PLANTE
Montreal
(wins for fourth straight time)

They Wear Parachutes When Jumping Out Of Planes, Don't They?

After being hit in the face with a puck during a game against the New York Rangers in New York's Madison Square Garden, Montreal Canadiens' Jacques Plante shocks fans by returning to the ice wearing a face mask which he designed himself, becoming the first goalie to do so during a regular season game.

GOLF CHAMPIONS

Professional Golfers Association
Bob Rosburg

Ladies Professional Golfers Association
Betsy Rawls

Women's National Amateur
Barbara McIntire

British Open
Gary Player
(Youngest winner in modern history)

Masters
Art Wall, Jr.
(Wins by one stroke with 72-hole score of 284)

U.S. Amateur
Jack Nicklaus
(Youngest winner in 50 years)

U.S. Open
MEN: **Billy Casper**
WOMEN: **Mary Kathryn "Mickey" Wright**
(Sets record by winning title two years in a row)

LEADING PROFESSIONAL MONEY WINNER
ART WALL, JR. (Approximately $50,000)

• After winning 63 tournaments over thirty years golfing legend **Ben Hogan** retires.

• The U.S. retains the Walker Cup defeating the British amateurs 9-3 in Scotland.

TENNIS

CHAMPIONS

U.S. OPEN (SINGLES)
Men: Neal A. Fraser (over Alejandro Olmedo)
Women: Maria Bueno (over Christine Truman)

WIMBLEDON
Men: Alejandro Olmedo (over Rod Laver)
Women: Maria Bueno (over Darlene Hard)

DAVIS CUP
In the deciding game played in Forest Hills, New York, Australia's Neale Fraser beats America's Barry MacKay 3-2 regaining the Davis Cup.

12-Year Old Romanian Ilie Nastase, Wins National Boys' Title.

PASSINGS
Tennis Hall of Fame member and record 8-time winner of the U.S. Women's Singles, **Molla Bjurstedt Mallory**, dies at 67.

FAMOUS BIRTHS

Danny Ainge
•
Earvin "Magic" Johnson
•
Florence Griffith Joyner
•
Ronnie Lott
•
John McEnroe
•
Jim McMahon

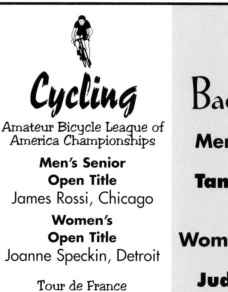

Cycling

Amateur Bicycle League of America Championships

Men's Senior Open Title
James Rossi, Chicago

Women's Open Title
Joanne Speckin, Detroit

Tour de France
Spain's **Federico Bahamontes** wins Europe's blue-ribbon event.

Badminton

Men's Singles Title
Tan Joe Hok
(Indonesia)

Women's Singles Title
Judy Devlin
(USA)

Pan-American Games

Swimming

15-year old Susan "Chris" von Saltza of Los Gatos High School in Santa Clara, California wins five gold medals.

Marathon

Groton, Connecticut teacher John Kelley scores outstanding victory.

Basketball

Men: United States
Women: United States

Gymnastics

Men:
(all around)
John Beckner, U.S.
(114.3 pts.)

Women:
(all around)
Ernestine Russell, Canada
(38.467 pts.)

Volleyball

Men: United States
Women: Brazil

Wrestling

AMATEUR ATHLETIC NATIONAL CHAMPIONS: Bill Kerslake keeps heavyweight crown and Terry McCann keeps the crown in the 125.5 lb. class.

Yachting

Peter Grant's "Nalu II," a 46-ft. sloop, wins the Transpacific race from Los Angeles, California to Honolulu, Hawaii.

Table Tennis

New York City's Bobby Gusikoff defeats Marty Reisman winning U.S. National Open Table Tennis championship and Susie Hoshi defeats Sharon Acton in the women's division.

New York City's Westminster Club Top Dog Award goes to Miniature Poodle champion **Fontclair Festoon**.

Anne Hone Rogers becomes **first woman dog trainer** to twice win the Westminster Kennel Club's Best Dog ribbon when her black Miniature Poodle **Tina** takes first prize.

Bobsledding

The United States gets its first international crown since 1950 when **ART TYLER** of Boston pilots his four-man sled to top honors in St. Moritz, Switzerland.

SIR HUGH STOCKWELL
Wins The World's
tiddlywinks
Championship In London.

PASSINGS

Perhaps the greatest billiards player in the history of the game, Willie Hoppe dies at age 71. He won his first championship at age 18 and was the three-cushion champion for nearly a half century.